KEYS OF GNOSIS

ROBERT BOLTON

KEYS OF GNOSIS

SOPHIA PERENNIS

HILLSDALE NY

First published in the USA
by Sophia Perennis
© Robert Bolton 2004

This book reconstructs
and further develops ideas which
were first introduced in the author's
The Logic of Spiritual Values, published 1996

Series editor: James R. Wetmore

For information, address:
Sophia Perennis, P.O. Box 611
Hillsdale NY 12529
sophiaperennis.com

Library of Congress Cataloging-in-Publication Data

Bolton, Robert (Robert A. N.)
Keys of gnosis / Robert Bolton.—1st ed.

p. cm.

ISBN 0 900588 83 7 (pbk: alk. paper)
1. Knowledge, Theory of. 2. Gnosticism. I. Title
BD181.B63 2001
299'.932—dc22   2004019296

CONTENTS

INTRODUCTION

MANY FAMILIAR VALUES, which might be thought to be just inherited social conditioning, can be shown to have hidden depths when examined in the light of metaphysical thought. Once it is realized that the everyday world depends on an unseen world with a reality of its own, values can be understood as the points at which this unseen world enters our awareness of the visible one, rather as the mountain tops of a submerged continent appear to us as islands.

The existence of such subtle realities cannot be ignored with impunity, and their hidden action is decisive in relation to the freedom and powers of activity which are possible for human beings. Consequently, this study will not evade or minimize the thorny subject of the relation between power and spirituality, under various aspects. Idealists nearly always deny that they could ever be power-gatherers on the grounds that power is never intentionally sought by them and that, on the contrary, they are making actual sacrifices. However, these answers are either naive or self-deceiving. The repression of awareness of certain aspects of one's motivation is so far from repressing its natural effects that it may well enable it to operate more freely. That the religions and power are closely connected is sufficiently proved by their ability to acquire huge material resources, and in their ability to influence politics.

To make this better understood, moral and religious values will be examined in an analytical manner, but in a way which will cut across the normal boundaries of academic study such as those of philosophy, theology, and psychology, so that our perception of their operation will not be artificially limited. Personal development is inevitably a process of empowerment among other things, but because this development is also a part of natural life, it is regarded as just a worldly concern by most traditional guides and teachers, who pass over its spiritual dimension. This is unfortunate because its place in the divine order of things can be shown to be indispensable. The question of its due recognition is even more relevant today when inhibitions against the natural have been generally removed.

To have power over the direction of one's life is in any case a universal desideratum, since it is relevant to all purposes from the most exalted to the most mundane. Without some measure of it, the fulfilment of all other desires appears to be only a form of escapism. It is at very least implicit in the ideals of religious teachings, despite their lack of direct reference to it. Another reason for this silence is that control over one's life is almost always popularly misunderstood in selfish and materialistic terms. Innumerable examples of worldly success show that one can be in control of one's life for certain purposes in one kind of society, though this only distracts attention from the central question of how to live authentically under any conditions.

This misunderstanding of personal power forms part of a near-universal modern inability to understand the meaning of the spiritual life whenever it takes forms which are not conducive to the usual practicalities. It is often seen as a form of anti-social selfishness, and an evasion of the only real obligations we can have, as though spiritual reality was but a faint shadow of the material world. Thus for modern minds, the highest ideal has become confined to that of sainthood, while that in turn has become confined to the moral qualities society is willing to recognize as sainthood. But besides this ideal, there is another, more inclusive one, that of the Adept, in whom sainthood is combined with knowledge and power. While this ideal is more demanding intellectually, in that it requires more than morality, it is also closer to things which we instinctively know to be meaningful. When the perspective of adepthood is ignored, the deepest self-knowledge is blocked and deformed, because we cannot understand what we really are unless we understand what we are capable of becoming. Here, the spiritual ideal must transcend the usual popular simplifications.

Many of those who hold religious beliefs understand this issue no more than do unbelievers, with the result that humanism continues to infiltrate modern religion. The problem is to explain how lives which are not notable by utilitarian criteria can still have a usefulness to the world beyond the views of materialism. For this purpose, a series of subjects will be brought together and related to the central theme of self-understanding. The reason why this is related to an apparently egotistical subject like that of power lies in the higher forms it can take.

There is an adage that knowledge is power, which is usually repeated as though it needed no explanation. But in real life it may not appear to be so, especially if the possession of it means membership of a minority with no special rights. However, even if it effected nothing directly, it can still free one from the power of collective ignorance. There is nothing worse than alliances of ignorance with power, and there are all too many such alliances in today's world. They rule most of all those who do not know enough to see ignorance as ignorance. At very least, then, knowledge is the antidote to the wrong kinds of power, such as have a way of draining legitimate power from their victims. The whole range of evils which afflict the human race reduces to the problem of increasing numbers of persons who lack power over their lives spiritually as much as materially, the two problems being closely related. There is something deeply unnatural about such helplessness because it does not come from our true nature, but rather from a blindness to that nature. Unless each successive generation can continue to overcome this blindness, it may not be possible to save civilization from barbarism.

To explain this more fully, it will be necessary to challenge a number of uncritically-accepted ideas about the nature of personal identity. This can be done by means of a number of key concepts which should make it impossible to return to certain common sense assumptions which are infected with materialism. The subjects treated will include such issues as: Do we know that there is a soul? What defines a human being? What is the most universal activity? What is the most universal law which applies to our lives? If there is such a thing as fate, can we get free of it?

The thought employed in the following chapters is of an inclusive kind, which effects a combination of reason with intuition. This is to prevent thought from falling into the extremes of either an analytical philosophy with no transcendental dimension, or a mystical thought which aims at transcendence without the theoretical principles which would allow an objective grasp of it. Metaphysical thought has essential things in common with both mystical and rationalistic thought without having any need to identify with either.

Popular or New Age mysticism and ultra-rationalism are a pair of opposites which, like most opposites, still have certain things in common. They both enshrine a negative attitude to the intellect, the one in the more passive manner of by-passing it as something unnecessary, and the other in the more active manner of denying it any access to non-physical reality. There is also a certain compatibility between them, owing to the fact that the materialist outlook is no more than minimally challenged by non-rational vindications of the transcendental. Those who see things in this way are not usually open to the idea that the intelligence belongs to both the natural and to the supernatural equally, and so are liable to take as limited a view of it as do materialists.

For a long time now, religion in the West has been polarized between a democratic kind of faith meant for simple believers, and divine mysteries so high that hardly anyone can claim to know much about them. The vital connecting region between them, that of metaphysical religion, is all but lost for orthodox purposes. Some of it has leaked away into the New Age movement, where it exists out of contact with the historical roots of civilization. Besides providing continuity, this metaphysical dimension of religion is the remedy for ignorance where it is most dangerous. In the world of common sense materialism, the self is always felt to be the ego and nothing else. Because of this, nearly all religions have to treat the self as simply the ego in the same way, in order to make contact with the cultures to which they are addressed. Nevertheless, the real self is much more than the ego, and this is where one must venture outside the usual boundaries, even though the grace of revealed religion remains necessary.

The true role and meaning of reason and the intellectual faculty will not be understood by those who keep to a materialistic idea like that of the self as ego alone, and for this reason, the following chapters will contain an attempt to shed some light on the meaning and purpose of the intellectual faculty. Even with common sense it can be seen that the rational mind is so made that it can govern its internal states. It is free, moreover, to increase the effectiveness of this governance without any apparent limit, so that it may become equal to even the strongest forces capable of deranging its thought and intention, even though the individual may not have control over anything else in the world. Far from being an individualistic dream of self-sufficiency, it is clear that this kind of power is essential to the very nature according to which we are formed, however little it may be realized in practice.

This is what connects the function of ideas with the realm of action and the capacity for action. Where this is blocked, all outward forms of action either atrophy or harden into routines or even pseudo-absolutes. The repression of this role of the intellect in modern thought shows an ignorance of the fact that it applies to workaday realities as well as to metaphysical ones. Despite this repression, mind is still efficacious enough to ensure that a civilization based on technology continues to function and that its industry and commerce are able to produce a living; in other words, we know that mind can connect with objective reality, and there is no reason why the range of this connection should be restricted of itself. The modern scepticism about reason is therefore a negation in the practical realm as much as in the theoretical. This can only smother the vitalizing force referred to above, and typifies a spiritually barren phase of civilization which future generations will be glad to forget when it has run its course.

The senses, the emotions, and the fantasy can be directly induced to operate in certain ways by the action of the relevant culture, but the activity of intelligence on the other hand is so dependent on self-activation that there is no point in trying to act upon it except by very indirect means. The rational soul, qua rational, is thus autonomous, not least because the all-important thing, the perception of the rational as such, cannot be supplied from without. This is not sufficiently realized where the intelligence is seen only as a tool for practical activities.

Such is the general outline of some leading features of the metaphysical standpoint which will be enlarged upon in the following chapters by the application of this form of thought to a series of subjects which are important both personally and spiritually. Chapters 1–7 are concerned with the nature of the self under various aspects, and chapters 8–13 with the self in relation to the providential order, and chapters 14 and 15 with the self in relation to God. Where both human nature and religious beliefs are involved equally, the abstract and the concrete can be brought into a specially close relation so as to show how speculative thought need not be solely a matter of abstraction. The problems of the world religions today, with their immersion in politics, arise in the wake of a neglect of metaphysical reality, and popular religion drifts into becoming a part of the cosmic process it should serve to overcome. Everything therefore depends on the liberation of the most universal beliefs and values from a popular and common sense idea of reality which is profoundly false.

1

THE NATURE
OF THE REAL SELF

WHOLE PERSON AND DUALITY

THE REAL SELF was always taken to be the immortal soul of the person, which was conceived to be the owner and controller of the body. This idea of the soul brings with it the traditional body-soul duality, which has been denied almost as a matter of principle over the past eighty years, as a result of a modern craving for simplification at any price, often with a sense of self-righteousness. In this way, the wisdom and experience of past ages was rejected, not because it was known to be wrong, but for ideological reasons. There is, of course, no simple or popular way of understanding how a union of soul and body could result in a single being with psychological unity. Nevertheless, the dualistic conception of the person remains necessary if self-knowledge is to get off ground level.

A great deal can be known about either soul or body in the abstract, because each of them manifests a general class of being. On the other hand, a whole person, regarded solely as a unity, is not knowable in this conceptual way, but only by acquaintance. This kind of self-unity is, besides, a spiritual dead-end, because all inner dynamism and growth come from an awareness of the actions and reactions between the soul and the person as a whole. Without this, there can only be a static sense of the self, vainly compensated by a mania for change and activity in everything else.

However, such has been the strength of the reaction against Dualism that the very existence of the soul now seems doubtful to the modern mind. If, in fact, the soul really is essential to the real self, the consequences of this for self-understanding must be crucial, and because of their potential importance, we need to find out which things in natural experience can reveal the soul's presence and activity to us. To do so, we shall have to examine a number of things which used to be routinely a part of philosophy, but which today are ignored because they are both clearly factual and incompatible with anti-dualist ideology. The facts involved may appear to have little to do with souls or self-knowledge, but if the reader will bear with what seems to be a digression, we shall arrive at a set of data which will point clearly to the function of the soul as the creative agent in our relations with the physical world. The importance of the phenomena reviewed below lies in their implications for the way in which the world and the soul subsist together to give rise to the self.

HOW NATURE IS DUAL

In 1673, Roemer did an experiment with light on the assumption that it moved with a finite velocity. It involved observations of Jupiter's four largest moons and the times of their disappearances and reappearances from behind that planet. By this means, he was able to calculate the velocity of light. Roemer showed that as light had a finite velocity, the eclipses of the moons were seen to happen at times which were later by a measurable amount, as the earth moved further away from Jupiter. This established the principle that a perception and the object perceived cannot simply be taken to be the same thing. Similarly with the stars we see, any one of which can be seen to be in a position it moved out of ages ago. If any given visual object is an object-at-time-t, that particular object no longer exists in the following moment. Relativity theory has taken the distinction between perceptions and their objects much further. Einstein's achievement 'consists essentially in this: he has succeeded in separating far more completely than hitherto the share of the observer and the share of external nature in the things we see happen.'[1]

1. See A. O. Lovejoy, *The Revolt Against Dualism.*

This major development of modern science underlines the perversity of modern philosophy in its determination to ignore the representational nature of our knowledge of the outside world. While Descartes is dethroned in the official forms of philosophy, he is nonetheless vindicated in the philosophy of science. His dualism has been called the cornerstone of the new physics, and quite reasonably, in view of the way in which modern scientific discoveries diverge ever more profoundly from anything open to sense-perception; and in view of the fact that a fundamental difference between perceptions and percepts is the very basis of relativity theory. Without the principle that the world of sense experience is a world of individual representation, natural science could not exist. Scientific thinkers may talk of closing the gap between representation and reality, but they cannot do anything effectual about it because the progress of science always means pushing knowledge further and further into realms beyond all normal experience.

Ordinary experience is filled with examples of the difference between what we experience and what we believe actually exists, so much so that it is wholly dominated by this. We constantly perceive square or rectangular objects as rhombuses or parallelograms, or parallels as converging, and circular forms like those of coins and cups are nearly always seen as elliptical. These things change their perceptible shapes as we move around them and grow bigger or smaller as we move nearer to or further from them. But so convinced are we that the real world consists mostly of things which have fixed shapes and sizes, and that man-made things are typically made rectangular or circular, that we become almost unconscious of our sensory evidence which keeps on contradicting these beliefs.

Similarly, we believe that the real world consists mostly of things which exist as continuously as we do ourselves, despite the fact that there is no direct sensory evidence for this. What our perceptions tell us would be just the opposite if we relied on them alone as the things around us appear, disappear, and reappear, more or less in sequence with the way we move ourselves and our center of attention. From an empirical point of view, the continuous existence of everything about us would be simply a piece of theory and not a basic assumption, let alone an experience. Consequently, no matter how closely our perceptions of the world may resemble the contents of that world, there is no way in which they can be literally the same things.

At this point I would add an argument which philosophers do not as a rule make use of, possibly because it is almost embarrassingly evident. This is the fact that every experience of our world necessarily takes the form of objects arranged in concentric circles or spheres, centered on our own body. Perception is thus Ptolemaic, so to speak, by its very nature. Since there is no way in which the objective world could really revolve about one's body, it follows that all perceptions of the world are private and personal representations of it.

From a more sophisticated point of view, our perceptions differ from their objects in an even more remarkable way, one which arises from our knowledge of the ways in which natural laws and causes operate. We constantly perceive things which can be shown to obey the laws of mechanics, optics and electricity, but we hardly ever reflect that our perceptions of these regular phenomena do not themselves obey any laws at all, and that neither are they the causes of anything else, even though we perceive them as caused by their objects. For example, Newton's laws of motion cannot govern the order of our perception of what moves, and still less motion in fantasy. Similarly, there are no naturally perceptible laws in the outside world unless we change our behavior to find them. Thus the Moon's phases appear only as a lawless jumble of shapes if the Moon is observed irregularly and without any special intention. Only if the observations are made with a regularity corresponding to the Moon's phases will we see the law of its phases. Such cases result from the fact that our sense data cannot be subject to natural laws while being also subject to our wills. All this would be impossible were there not a fundamental difference between the world in itself and our representations of it. Should there be any doubt about the absence of causal capacity in our mental impressions, one need only consider whether one's brain is ever heated by mental impressions of fire, or whether a mental fire needs to be extinguished with mental water.

Though mental impressions have no causal power, they can still be the occasions of our having emotional states about them, but that depends on the disposition of our will, and so these events must differ according to the person involved. This is wholly different from the uniformity of natural causes. Our impressions are in fact largely ruled by our will, which selects them, along with their frequency and duration. Our mental impressions of natural processes are typically lacking in the continuity, order, and self-continuation of those phenomena.

From this it is no very long deduction to the conclusion that scientific thought could never have begun before man had learned to distinguish between representations of actual things and the empty representations of dreams, fantasies and hallucinations. Anti-dualistic thought would abolish this division by putting back all these 'wild data' into nature, regardless of whether science could survive it. This is in defiance of the fact that conscious beings live, almost by definition, outside their bodies, and the only way in which they can do so is by external things being made present inwardly through representations. Though the latter are spatial in form, that is only because they correspond to physical space while they themselves do not occupy any public space at all, in keeping with their lack of physical causality. For example, a hundred persons viewing the interior of a meeting-hall have a hundred representations of it which all together take up no space in the hall itself.

This points to a 'one-way' relation between our impressions and their objects inasmuch as the latter cause them, whereas the impressions do not exert any reciprocal action. They are endlessly multiplied in more or less the same form in the experience of different observers of the same objects, and in each case they form part of a separate inner world. The only alternative to this endless multiplication of the outside world would be that objects be in many different places at the same time. Real objects would have to travel with magical speeds, so as to form the different combinations of them we have in our minds, if experience had to be explained in terms of originals and not representations.

Another consequence of unmediated, or non-representational experience, if there were such a thing, is that it would make error impossible. Direct grasp of the original objects of perception would mean sensory infallibility. It should be noted that there is in fact no difference between veridical perceptions and illusory ones *qua representations*, but only in the way in which they relate to what is known already. Veridical perceptions correspond to their objects, whereas fantasies, illusions, or 'wild data' do not correspond to them, and therefore not to any retinal images either.

The nature of our knowledge of the physical world in the light of the above is summed up by A. O. Lovejoy as follows:

> Essentially, knowing is a phenomenon by which the simple location of things is circumvented without being annulled. Upon any metaphysical theory deserving of serious consideration, reality is an aggregate of *partes extra partes*. Every particular is in its own time, or in its own place ... they do not escape from their reciprocal exclusiveness ... and the being-known of a thing is its getting reported where it does not exist—and its getting reported there as existing at the locus or region in which it does not exist.[2]

Lovejoy points out a specially decisive field in which Dualism is unavoidable, this being memory. Although its implications are strangely neglected by most philosophers, the distinction between the object and our representation of it stands out more clearly here than anywhere else: 'to remember is to be aware of the difference between the present image and the event recalled.' One could not deny this without denying the existence of memory itself. Doubts about the relevance of Descartes' *cogito ergo sum* could be settled, as Lovejoy shows, by the fact that the mere passage of time continually transforms it into *memini ergo fui*, something much less open to sceptical attack. In any case, our ability to recollect the recent past plays a crucial part in our experience of the present. So much of what one sees going on at any given time would mean nothing to anyone without a recollection of what had been going on one or two minutes before then.

The upshot of this is that if there were such a thing as unmediated experience at a given time, its status as present experience would depend so largely on memory content, which is dualistic by definition, that no true alternative to representation would result. The

2. *The Revolt Against Dualism*, chap. 9.

interweaving of past with present also extends into the future, since our ability to think constructively in practical ways depends wholly on whether we can think effectively about future events. But our future or intended activities have never been objects of present experience, whence here again there is no room for doubt as to the duality between them and our present thoughts about them. In all such cases, the object must be present vicariously or not at all; what has never been experienced is, if possible, even less accessible than things now past. The knowledge of things past and future merges continuously with present experience, showing how practical needs do not depend on unmediated experience, any more than do theoretical ones.

REAL SELF AND FALSE SELF.

At this stage it need not take long to indicate the outcome of the facts instanced so far. The world about us is neither more nor less than our private and personal representation of the objective world. In view of the difference between these two realities, we infer the existence of a third reality in which they can be related so as to form a common system, one which both adapts and contains the world as the individual knows it. Such is precisely what the soul is understood to mean. On this basis, the existence of the soul is as sure as the facts of representation, this being both the generator and the medium of the represented form of the world one knows. Because of their intimate connection with the soul, the publicly-accessible facts of representation have a cause which is our own individual being. The real self, or soul, is thus a sphere of consciousness which contains the physical universe in its own mode, and many more subtle realities besides. While man is not unique among living creatures in having a soul with this property, he is unique inasmuch as the human soul is rational and self-aware, as well as object-aware.

The psychological and cultural context of this subject is worthy of consideration, not least because of a prevalent inclination to deny the validity of this kind of analysis. The present-day conception of the person as a physical reality forming part of a physical world which is supposedly known in an immediate manner, has the effect of maximizing the power of the environment over the individual for those who believe in it. At the same time, this view of the person, with its denial of the inward being, serves to suppress the differences between individuals, since what we are as observable egos at any given time is very limited in comparison with the real self. This goes with a hostility to both privacy and superiority, and these things are connected by the reality of the individual, which such thinking would deny. At the same time, the natural sciences, with their aim of reducing everything to the level of physical facts, and a philosophy which equates persons with their observable egos, form the ideological background to modern attitudes.

But although the methods used are ultra-rationalistic, the motivation behind them is unmistakably passional, not to mention the fact that its wilful ignoring of the distinction between objective reality and representation is almost a guarantee of delusion. The quasi-mystical tendency which Lovejoy calls 'dyophobia', if seriously believed in, implies a degree of resistance to manifest realities which by rights should be a subject for psychoanalysis rather than for philosophy. It could be said that modern attempts to escape representation seem to be moved by a belief that if the contents of experience were arranged with enough ingenuity, it could cease to be representation. The real mistake here is to think that duality can be overcome on its own level, which is done by materialists who think there is no level but the material one. But if that should be impossible, it may yet be overcome elsewhere; that, in fact, is what Platonism is largely concerned with. But this answer depends on the idea of different levels of being.

The difference between perception and reality brings us to the idea of the real self as the soul, which would be the container of our world-representation, and this would form a complete counterpart to the common sense idea of a bodily self living and moving in space and time with other physical entities. This does not mean that the latter idea is false in itself, however, because it only becomes an illusion when it is taken to be exclusively true. The real self is rather the combination of the physical self of common sense and the soul with its world representation. This is a far more complete reality, one which can be thought, but not grasped by the imagination, however, since it goes far beyond the limits of the common sense self or ego.

The price of this disregard of the real self is the typical misconception of the whole self as being just one more item among all the other objects in its own field of representation. But once the truth about the real self is understood, it can be seen that the 'choir of heaven and all the furniture of earth' are not as alien to the self as they appear to be for naive or ego-centered perception. Instead, the objective world is known to have a form which results as much from its adaptation to our own powers of cognition, as from its objective nature. For this reason, the vastness of the manifest world is also a reflection of our own larger self, in which the ego and its environment are enclosed like a seed in a fruit.

Visionary and fictional accounts of the world occupy as much and as little of the real self as does the physical universe, while the self which could be said to be relatively nothing could therefore only be the ego, not the soul. In traditional mystical writings, therefore, the 'self' which is often said to be 'nothing' is invariably the ego, because in earlier times there was still no technical terminology for the real self. We thus have a vastly extended range of meaning for the individual once he or she no longer has to be equated with the ego alone.

This conclusion is completely in line with what has been said about the soul by the founders of Western tradition, as where Plotinus says:

> But soul is not in the universe, on the contrary the universe is in the Soul; bodily substance is not a place to the Soul; Soul is contained in Intellectual-Principle and is the container of body.[3]

The intellectual principle is in turn contained by God, so that the soul both contains and is contained in a hierarchy of being and reality. By representing physical reality to itself, the soul transposes physical reality onto the psychic level, upon which it can be an object for the higher-order beings whose nature is purely spiritual. At the same time, the consciousness of the individual person is the fulcrum on which all this turns: every object is the counterpart of a subject.

---

3. Plotinus, *Enneads*, v, 5, 9.

Finally, there is a criticism of representation which states that if we have to have representations to mediate between our minds and physical realities, there must result an infinite regress. Such criticisms assume that we can never grasp the original of anything, which Dualists do not try to maintain. Our first representation of the outside world is a reality in its own way, it is said, and so then we should need a second representation to know it, and then a third one to know the second, and so on.

This objection is mistaken because Dualism only implies that we do not have direct knowledge of the material world, while it affirms that we do directly apprehend mental realities like representations. If it should be asked why, if we can know mental realities directly, we should not be able to know everything else in the same way, we need only refer to a basic argument for representation: that if one had the true originals of sense-objects, they could not be accessible for anyone else at the same time.

2

A PRIMARY CERTAINTY

CERTAINTY IN THE SELF

Given the part played by the soul in the real self, we can now consider it from a different angle so as to see what manner of certainty the self can provide from within, that is, in a way not dependent on sensation. The presence of the soul as such was deduced from an analysis of our relation to the outside world, though this itself does not show whether the soul by its own nature can achieve certainty about itself through itself alone. Such a certainty would be a foundation for many others like it, in accordance with the principle that when something is established as a possibility, other things in the same category will be possible as well.

This need for self-certainty was for a long time answered by Descartes' *cogito* argument, which is now generally found unacceptable because it formed part of an extreme Dualist position which would divide body and soul from one another by an inexplicable gulf. Such a radical separation would make it impossible to explain the interaction between body and soul. This is, to some degree, responsible for the modern resistance to the very idea of the soul, since it became identified with the Cartesian conception. The idea that two substances which have nothing in common should be able to form a single person is a barrier to the understanding which detracts from what may be made known about the soul, therefore, so Descartes gives with one hand and takes with the other, so to speak.

Consequently, this subject needs to be detached from the reaction against Descartes by tracing it back to the way it was understood in earlier times. There are two questions here, those of interaction and of the basic certainty that the essence of our understanding is logically prior to any knowledge of the sense world.

Both the body-soul relation and the *cogito* argument have a history extending back to antiquity, the former in Plato's philosophy, and the latter in that of St. Augustine. For Plato, the soul is a distinct substance, joined to the body and in control of it, and capable of existing without the body. In the same way, he conceived the eternal Forms of the things we perceive as subsisting independently of the material things in which they are manifest. Thus the body was related to the soul by being the material instantiation of it, rather as a circular object is an instantiation of the Circle itself. The properties of the body were therefore a recapitulation on the physical level of the properties of the soul, which were their causes.

Here, Plato inverted the order of common sense, giving the fullest reality to souls and Forms, while bodies were dependent reflections of them. This makes the vital difference that the action of soul on body cannot be taken to be the supposed action of an abstract upon a concrete. The stark opposition between them is in principle solved in a way which allows a primary concreteness to the soul, from whence the body is in a sense projected.

Something of this idea was taken up by Descartes, except that he did not include Plato's account of the body and of the material world which went with it. It is this omission more than anything else which has brought the relation of body and soul into difficulties. By adopting the separate natures of body and soul while retaining the materialistic common sense idea of the outside world, Descartes exposed the idea of the soul to damaging criticisms which really apply only to his philosophy.

Moreover, the simple dichotomy of body and soul is in certain respects transcended by the later developments of Neoplatonism, where the full complexity of the soul's role as 'Form of the body' is worked out. This kind of philosophy excludes the idea of an absolute difference between soul and body in other ways as well, notably in regard to the motion involved in both mental and physical activity. The soul is fully conversant with space and time, deploying its activity according to them, while having besides its own equivalent of motion, as its condition is necessarily temporal. Sharing motion and relatedness to space and time with corporeal things, the soul is able to impart motion to the latter, and in this respect they clearly have something in common, even for common sense. The Platonic view of the creation of the soul as the blending of Being with Becoming highlights just this function of mediator between the unchanging Forms and mutable and mobile material things.

THE ORIGINAL COGITO ARGUMENT

This, however, is secondary to the main subject, that of self-certainty, and the arguments from whence the idea of it originates. The Cartesian *cogito* argument was anticipated in the works of St Augustine, who, like Descartes, was concerned with refuting scepticism. The main thrust of his arguments is that absolute doubt is self-contradictory because one cannot rationally have doubts about anything unless one first knows something; one cannot complain of the dark unless one first knows what light is. Accordingly, a way is sought to justify the idea that the soul is 'certain that it alone is the only thing of which it is certain,' the only thing, that is, in the realm of individual existents. This conclusion would harmonize with what was said earlier about representation, because it is only in self-knowledge that the individual can be known without it.

Unlike Descartes, Augustine does not try to make the *existence* of the individual the final result. Instead, he starts with it, and uses it to develop the idea of metaphysical certainty, that is, a knowledge generated by the power of rational thought alone. One example of argument used takes the knowledge that we exist, live, know, and desire to know, as defining a region which is *per se* beyond the reach of sceptical attack.

Elsewhere, he examines doubt as such:

If it is certain that you do indeed have doubts, inquire whence comes that certainty. It will never occur to you to imagine that it comes from the light of the Sun but rather from that 'true light which lighteth every man that cometh into the world.' It cannot be seen with these eyes, nor with the eyes which seem to see the phantasms of the brain, but with those eyes that can only say to phantasms: You are not the thing I am seeking. . . . Everyone who knows that he has doubts knows with certainty that something is true, namely, that he doubts. He is certain, therefore, about a truth.[1]

But as there cannot be an instance of anything without the universal reality it depends on, it follows that: 'no one ought to have doubts about the truth, even if doubts arise for him from every quarter.'[2]

In the midst of all the deceptions and half-lights of experience, therefore, there is an indestructible standard of truth in the mind's own working by which we know where and how we are deceived. Our very doubts make us aware of this truth, just as black recalls white, or darkness, light. Instead of deriving the fact that one exists from the certainty of one's thinking, Augustine starts with existence and the fact that we know it, and from thence derives a nucleus of unassailable certainties which are the basis of *a priori* knowledge. They are, we are told, known in a manner superior to that of sense-perception, whence they cannot be made into deceptions.

This form of the Cogito argument likewise disposes of the doubt as to whether we are dreaming, because even if we are dreaming, we can still know ourselves to be alive, and know that we are trying to avoid deception. The existence of such self-reflexive knowledge is not compatible with the sense-bound nature of the dream state. In short, the basic certainties of existing, living and knowing are the grounds for a knowledge which has no intrinsic limits, whether from dreams or any other natural force:

> For he who says: 'I know that I live,' says that he knows one thing; if he were then to say 'I know that I know that I live,' there are already two things, but that he knows these two is to know a third thing; and so he can add a fourth and a fifth, and innumerable more.[3]

This kind of knowledge shows that the real self must be more than a container of sensory representations. As an intellect, it has certainties which are part of its essence, arising from its existing, living and knowing.

1. Augustine, *True Religion*, XXIX.
2. Ibid.
3. Augustine, *The Trinity*, bk. 15, chap. 12.

This inherent knowledge is the counterpart to our sensory knowledge of the outside world, and means that the mind is not wholly enclosed in the world of sense perception, but has the key to a realm of immediate knowledge beyond the duality of subject and object peculiar to the senses.

OVERCOMING REPRESENTATION

If there is no escape from representation on its own sensory level, therefore, this does not mean that there is no escape from it at all. The mind is in direct contact with its own processes and ideas and this is far from meaning that it has only a world of private subjectivity. The mental realm opens out into a counterworld of universal ideas whose relations the mind can grasp and thereby grasp the formative principles which underlie the sensory world. Far from being a confinement of the mind, this means that its activity can expand into an unlimited realm of universal truths which are far more surely knowable than anything deriving from sensation. The implication behind this is that the physically manifest realities, of which the soul forms its representations, are in many cases less real than the ideal realities which are known directly. The latter are the eternal and universal basis of their temporal and localized instantiations in the sense world.

Thus sensations do not become true perceptions until sensation and intellectual conception function together, the mind as it were 'reading' the intelligible originals of the *sensa* which it has representations of. Failing this, there is only the unprocessed sensation we receive when we absentmindedly see or hear things without interest. There is no use in the sensation 'coming in' if the activity of mind does not 'go out' to meet it and join it to its Form. The Forms of material things, along with principles and values such as truth, order, proportion, equality, harmony, virtue, have the peculiarity that, besides being native to the soul of the knower, they are in some sense 'older' than the universe of sense. They are the ideational patterns fixed from eternity, in accordance with which innumerable finite and temporal worlds come into being, which are real in proportion to the adequacy with which they represent these ideal realities.

What happens then, when we deduce true statements, is that we become distinctly conscious of new combinations of ideas according to the laws by which they can or cannot combine, which before we knew only confusedly. Acts of understanding are acts of recollection on this level, and they are always original and novel for the individual, regardless of how many others may have achieved the same insight before. Even the means by which it is achieved, whether by a direct study of facts or of written accounts of it, is a relative and secondary matter compared with the comprehension of truth itself.

THE THEORY OF RIGHT AND WRONG

The idea of the real self as the combination of the ego with a soul which is characterized by its own unique representation of the world is similar to the idea of the self in Leibniz' *Monadology*, while also differing from it inasmuch as it retains the existence of the objective world as the source of the representations we make of it.

Among the consequences of this idea is a means of answering the perennial question as to what moral right and wrong are in themselves. Morally significant actions and attitudes involve a special class of interactions between the self or soul and the contents of its world. This idea of the soul dictates a fundamental difference in degrees of reality between itself and any part of its contents. The latter are always as accidents in relation to the soul as substance, to use the Scholastic terms. There is no common measure between the soul and its world-representations.

Man's powers of self-awareness are usually not active enough to prevent his effectively putting the self on the same, or even lower, level than that of the objects in his world. This is the metaphysical mistake which can account for a great range of moral wrongs. Morally wrong behavior can thus be said to arise whenever the natural desires and aversions turn into uncontrollable cravings, compulsions and hatreds which both result from a blindness to the real self, and reinforce it. While things can be desired or rejected in ways which respect the ontological divide between them and the self which cognizes them, the moral danger is always that this limitation will be ignored through inattention.

A world in which many of its represented contents (when not connected with the higher values) are felt to be as important, or more important, than the self in which they exist can seem richer or more exciting than one in which the central difference in value is observed. This greater richness nevertheless results from an illusion, a pretended making-equal of things which can never be equal in reality. The alternatives are therefore those of directing the will at a real possibility or of directing it at an ultimate impossibility.

In the latter case, one blindly identifies with some portion of the 'cosmic illusion' wherein the person sees himself or herself solely as one *relatum* among other *relata*. This is not a moral wrong in itself, but is the basis of all such wrongs, even though it does not include cases where relationships contain true values. Traditional strictures against 'the world' which are usually meaningless to modern minds can be made perfectly intelligible on this basis. The real sense of this word 'world' is a certain kind of illusion. There is a well-known spiritual practice which owes its effectiveness to this difference of level between the knower and the known, namely, the deliberate emptying of the mind by concentrating on a single object. This makes manifest the independent reality of the soul in relation to its contents or representations.

What has been argued so far, is that the real self is primarily the soul, and that it has a self-knowledge inherent in its own workings, from whence an unlimited number of ideas or objective universals can be known independently of sensation. In this property, we have the answer to problems inherent in the representational nature of the world about us. While that nature cannot be overcome on its own level, despite what some modern philosophers suppose, it can be transcended in conceptual thought which does not depend on sensation for its truth.

What is lacking in this account of human identity is a property which would differentiate human beings from all other forms of life which perceive the material world in ways similar to our own, and which are similarly ensouled. When it is clear what defines the human soul among the general order of souls, we shall be better able to understand the values based on it.

3

THE DEFINING PRINCIPLE

NARROWING THE DEFINITION

We shall not be able to elaborate further on the precept 'know thyself' until we can find a means of defining the human state, since soul and simple self-identity do not suffice for this, essential as they are. Without something more precise, what we know of ourselves will not have an adequate foundation. The chief difficulty here lies in the very excess of possible criteria by which man can define or at least distinguish himself, such as Political Animal, or Religious Being, or creature which can laugh or cry. We need to find which one among them has a universality not shared by the others, and which is also specific enough to apply only to man.

The first requirement of the definition is that it should depend on something which is not shared by any other species. It must be manifest in an activity which is not merely unique to man, like laughter, but has a direct relation to all his activities. The defining property of a particular tuning fork, for example, lies in the precise note it makes, and not in the properties it has in common with other tuning forks. This implies that we cannot use such criteria as preying on one's own species, making and using tools, or even producing works of art. None of these could form part of the purpose of life for all persons, but we come nearer the mark when the use of speech is taken as a definition. The latter is to a special degree determined by reason, and is free from the restrictions that apply to most of the others. As reason in a manifest form, it is something which is not merely an option for us, besides being peculiar to human life, and it meets the condition of being needful for all kinds of activity. In view of this, it can be seen to support a definition of the human state which is neither too restricted nor too extended, and it has the suitability of properties like being able to walk in an upright posture, without their limitations.

A common misunderstanding that arises in connection with reason or rationality is owing to the manifest prevalence of irrationality in human life. If a large part of mankind behaves irrationally much or most of the time, it may seem that the necessary universality of reason would not be consistent with our making a defining principle of it. However, a definition can be based on something which happens to be true of the majority, no matter how accidentally or inessentially; or it can be based on what human beings essentially are, no matter how few may manifest it to any great extent. On the one hand, we may be characterized as being in a fallen state which is reflected in the manifest condition of the human race as a whole, whereas, more philosophically, we may disregard the numbers involved and concentrate on what lies behind the appearances. Thus man as a physical being could be defined by his eyesight, even in a world where everyone was either blind or had very defective eyesight, on the grounds that the definition of a species must be in terms of only its complete specimens. In this way we have the advantage of a definition which reaches the essence of the being, cutting through the appearances.

The uniqueness of rational intelligence in man is not affected by any of the supposed evidence for intelligence in the behavior of certain animal species either, because no amount of actions for which we would have to use reason could suffice to release the consciousness of animals from their absorption in the functions of their senses, even under direct pressure from human trainers. The possession of reason, as opposed to the performance of actions in which reason can see a reflection of itself, must also comprise rational processes pursued for the sake of truth alone. Without this condition, examples of supposed intelligence in animals result from the intelligence of their observers, and reveal only the animals' powers of adaptation and survival, along with the apparatus of instinct.

Until modern times, it would not have been necessary to emphasize the distinction between reason as a selfconsciously directed mental activity, and as a behavioral attribute of creatures not even aware of its presence, but today the accumulation of scientific observations has confused the issue too much for it to be passed over. What may clarify it further is the fact that while a pocket calculator produces results which would signify far more intelligence than does the behavior of even the most intelligent animal, no one thinks that such devices have any intelligence of their own. This kind of argument was first used by Pascal, and the essential issue remains the same.

While human beings share implicitly in nearly all the attributes of the animal creation, the reverse is not the case: none of the attributes of sense, emotion, instinct or even imagination can serve by themselves alone to distinguish the human state from the animal, or to define it, therefore. Without the presence of reason and rationality these things are ineffectual. Nevertheless, a definition of the human state based on reason, namely, that we are human to the extent that we are rational in practical or theoretical ways or both, is easily able to cause misunderstandings. This equation of humanity or manhood with rationality has given rise to the caricature of the cold logician who is half man and half machine, because the supremacy of reason among our powers is nearly always mistaken for an absurd attempt to rid oneself of everything except reason. Such a conclusion is as perverse as a supposition that the establishment of a government meant the expulsion of everyone from the country except the members of the government.

Should this definition of the human state appear too simple or too narrow, it should be realized that any apparent enrichment of the definition could only be at the expense of our ability to prove it. It will in any case be resisted by both the groups referred to earlier, those who seek the transcendent without logic, and those who pursue logical thought but deny transcendence. The conclusion just indicated here is thus liable to be disputed for contrary reasons, namely, for being too mundane and for being too spiritualistic. As the same path cannot be too wide and too narrow at the same time, the clearest implication is that this is a golden mean between two false extremes.

THE CENTRALITY OF REASON

Rationality throws light on the most varied issues, including that of the equality, or inequality, of men and women. Such issues are necessarily insoluble when there is no agreed definition of the human as such. In the light of the definition in terms of reason, the real issue can be seen to be about the relative superiority of two kinds of being, neither of which is fully human because of the naturalistic and non-rational ways in which their natures are understood, or rather misunderstood. Conversely, the definition used here is universal enough to be valid for women and men, and in this case, the only real inequalities will be relative to the common ideal. Real equality between persons would thus consist in an equal participation in a universal reality which does not harm individual differences.

Aristotle does not exaggerate when he argues that it would be intolerable if a hand or foot were to have a specific function while man himself did not, and so was useless.[1] In fact this would be the case if he were to be defined in terms of functions shared by innumerable other species. He would then be the most purposeless of the animals, and he would have no moral justification for his use of other creatures. If this were actually the case, the apparently purposeful properties of the nonhuman natural order would be as illusory in fact as they appear to be for natural science, if they were thought to culminate in the human race. Only through reason does mankind have a purpose which is the culmination of all purposes which are solely natural or biological.

The less the rational potentiality is realized, the more life will appear to be objectively purposeless, since untruths as well as truths always project themselves onto one's representation of the world if they are held consistently. Because reason is universal, and so common to both nature and the supernatural, sub-rational purposes remain trapped in the natural, and have no means of connecting with the world of the spirit. The denial of a universally objective purpose therefore opens the way to a swarm of invented purposes which, being mere creatures of the will, can only give rise to conflicts, both

---

1. Aristotle, *Nichomachean Ethics*, bk.1, 1097B, 30.

in the individual and in society. In spite of this, there is a belief that it is better to be able to invent purposes than to have a purpose which is specific to mankind, on the grounds that this would give us greater freedom. But the nemesis of this is that invented purposes always decline into the trivial, and the trivial undermines the will to live, along with the alleged freedom. Meaningful purpose must be founded on something both absolute and part of the self.

The human state has been conceived from ancient times as being a microcosm, and some confirmation of this idea can be found in the present subject, since the reasoning power which is specific to us implies the possession of an inner world which is not simply an extension of the material world, or the macrocosm. In addition to this, reason holds a central position in relation to nature, one which is equal in potentia to the entire range of data which the external world can confront us with. It can be shown that the properties of the remotest star belong as much within the reach of reason as do the least events closest to us; no phenomenon is any further from reason than another, as reason transcends both space and time. The nature of man as a microcosm thus appears as a 'one' which is effectively a counterpoise to the whole range of the many. Human minds are all alike in having this property, however much they may differ in the degree to which this is consciously realized.

At the beginning of life, we seem to have only the external world, with little awareness of self, and it is noteworthy that the acquisition of control over one's position in the world comes in proportion to the development of self-awareness. Until man possesses both the inner and the outer worlds, he does not really possess either, and this depends on a process of individuation in which the self is knowingly separated from the not-self. Paradoxically for common sense, then, control over the external world follows a disengagement of the sense of self from it, which Jung has called 'the dissolution of *participation mystique*.' At the same time, this development requires a conversion of vaguely intuitive beliefs into clearly-known ones, because the problem with common sense is that its ideas are confused, rather than simply false. Logically-founded truths are essentially descriptions in logical form of ideas which are present to the intellect or 'eye of the soul'. Metaphysical proof is therefore always logical, but it is never solely logical or wholly dependent on logic. Reasoning reaches its object like a ray of light but, like a ray, cannot determine its own direction. The role of intellect is essential here, with its relation to the intrinsic values of things prior to their perceived relations in the world. The extent of its presence or absence is what decides whether the use of reason will serve to draw the mind into the realm of the spirit, or whether it will draw it more deeply into the material world. Because it is not specifically natural or supernatural, it is necessarily a two-edged weapon, a fact which modern philosophy nearly always ignores.

A QUESTION OF PROOF

When a stricter proof is sought for the definition of the human being on the basis of reason, it will be enough to follow the course already indicated, that of excluding what man has in common with other creatures on the one hand, and things which are peculiar to but not essential to him, on the other. That reason must lie at the end of this process of elimination can be made more clear by a kind of mathematical approach which would start by assuming the proposed conclusion to be untrue. Let it be supposed that the real definition of the human lay in some other reality X, and that a proof to this effect has been given. This proof must be taken to be according to reason or to some direct observation. If it were logical, we should reach the conclusion that reason makes itself secondary or subordinate to something more essential than itself in the human state. But this would mean that this essential reality X was not able of itself to determine its own status, while reason, which could do so, puts itself second or lower in relation to it.

This is not the same as reason's ability to judge itself subordinate to some other beings, such as God or the angelic intelligences, because it is a question confined to the composition of the person, not to anything outside him. It is one thing for reason to conclude itself to be subordinate to a greater reality in the universe, and quite another to deny its own supremacy in the one substance where it has unmediated knowledge; the former case is self-consistent while the latter is self-contradictory.

When we speak of the intelligence as reason, it does not make much difference in this case whether it is reason with or without intellect, as its position as a governing principle is not affected by its spheres of application. As for why reason cannot be challenged for first place by other faculties, this can be seen more clearly from a comparison between the intelligence and the other elements which make up the personality, as in what follows.

REASON AND INTELLIGENCE

The conclusion as to the position of reason, or more generally, intelligence, among the faculties of the human microcosm can best be completed by a comparison between them which appears in the writings of Proclus. On the one hand, reason and intellect know themselves and all the other faculties as well, such as imagination, sense, and emotion. But on the other hand, imagination, sense, and emotion have of themselves no knowledge of intellect or reason, since their unbounded scope is only unlimited on a phenomenal level; they can only 'know' things in union with reason. This is why they cannot be said even to know themselves, since knowledge of images, sensations or anything phenomenal requires something essentially other than images and sensations to make them self-aware. Their supposed self-knowledge can therefore be only a borrowed one. Without reason and intellect, they would yield nothing more than what they amount to in the consciousness of animals. Just as in the external world man knows the animals while they do not know him, so in our inner world the intelligence knows the other faculties, but not vice-versa.

This comparison implies a 'one-way' relationship between the intelligence and the other faculties, and it is one which determines their relative status within the individual soul with a mathematical finality. While this definition of the human state concentrates on the aspect of reason rather than intellect, this is only because reason is the most practically accessible part of the intelligence. The real self was first defined on a basis of soul, but its limitation as a definition was owing to the fact that other forms of life are also ensouled. However, in the light of what has been argued here, it is possible to see a

new depth of meaning in the traditional conception of man as rational soul. Given the defining principle, it will not be too long a step to
determine the kind of activity which gives meaning and direction to
the life as a whole.

What has been said about reason and intellect follows the distinction between *dianoia* and *nous* in classical philosophy, which needs
to be pointed out because the intelligence has become more and
more equated with reason alone in modern times. Intellect, with the
higher intuition of the mind, is thereby ignored, despite the fact that
the same distinction in the intelligence has been rediscovered in
modern psychology, as appears in the work of Erich Fromm. Only
his terminology is both different and confused, as what has been
called reason here is called intelligence by Fromm, and what has
been called intellect, Fromm oddly calls reason:

> Intelligence is man's tool for attaining practical goals with the
> aim of discovering those aspects of things the knowledge of
> which is necessary for manipulating them.

He then indicates the limitations of his 'intelligence' (reason), in
that even the delusions of paranoiacs can be perfectly rational. This
faculty is then compared with the other part of the intelligence:

> Reason (i.e., intellect) involves a third dimension, that of depth,
> which reaches to the essence of things and processes. While rea-
> son is not divorced from the practical aims of life, it is not a mere
> tool for immediate action. Its function is to know, to under-
> stand, to grasp, to relate to things by comprehending them. It
> penetrates through the surface of things in order to discover
> their essence, their hidden relationships and deeper meanings,
> their 'reason.' It is, as it were, not two-dimensional but 'perspec-
> tivistic', to use Nietzsche's term, i.e., it grasps all conceivable per-
> spectives and dimensions, not only the practically relevant ones.[2]

Despite the confusion of terminology, this is an excellent account of
what has always been understood about the two 'wings' of the intelligence, and is full of implications for what follows.

2. Erich Fromm, *Man For Himself,* chap. III, 3b.

4

A UNIVERSAL ACTIVITY

HUMAN AND ANIMAL CONSCIOUSNESS

This subject is best approached by extending what has been said concerning man as a microcosm and the way in which it implies his uniqueness in relation to the whole natural order. When we compare the individuality of non-human beings with our own, the difference is not in degree of individuality but in the basis of it. In one sense, animal individuality is stronger than most human examples of it because the animal is essentially an instance of a species, so that it can only represent a pure type. Invariable conformity to the same norms was what made the animals symbolize divinity to the Egyptians. But the price of this assured identity is the limitation of consciousness to being solely an instrument for interaction with the environment from whence it is powerless to emerge; a perfect fit with a finite set of conditions means ultimate inseparability from them, and therefore no individual destiny

There are two ways in which human nature contrasts with this. Firstly, man can be fully an individual on the mental level as well as on the psycho-physical, since his intelligence has a potential equivalence to the entire content of the world, so that his nature cannot be fixed by any specialized set of functions like an animal's. Secondly, this kind of individuality admits of many degrees, because it has to be acquired by a long process of learning and development. While animal individuality is complete from the start, and thereby unalterable, the human form of it is in certain respects weaker because of its dependence on learning. One could say that an animal has to be what it is, while man has to become what he is, failing which he may remain with a consciousness as fatally entangled in the macrocosm as any animal, a condition which the greater complexity of human consciousness can only aggravate. This comparison therefore does not mean that failure in this regard implies any lack of intelligence, as popularly understood, at least. The extent to which the intelligence as reasoning power can be developed for the purpose of dealing with the environment is in no way tied to its development in the intellectual dimension, just as no amount of advance on the horizontal can cause the least advance in the vertical. Nevertheless, the intelligence is equally a part of the natural and the supernatural.

It is in the mystery of inwardness that we encounter the essential purpose of the intelligence, as opposed to the invented purposes of the world. The salient facts of animal consciousness enable us to see by way of contrast that an essential property of human consciousness lies in its power to initiate and direct its activities independently of external forces, and so be able to form itself into a conscious unity on the psychical level to match that of the physical being, which would otherwise make the mind a mere extension of itself. This involves an essential property of intelligence, as opposed to the other faculties, that of self-activation.

This property in itself is liable to energize activity on any level, since it can equally well inform reason's application to external matters, or lead one to follow the light of intellectual intuition in the direction of its source. However, when the mind is involved in practicalities, its self-activation is not as free as it is in relation to intellect, because in the outside world it necessarily encounters conditions and events over which it has no control. Conversely, in relation to intellect, the question of control does not arise, because things of an alien nature are not involved.

The implications of this are negative for some modern philosophies which take the mind's involvement in the *accidentalia* of time and space as though they were normative for it. Such notions emanate from Existentialist sources as much as from those of Empiricism and Positivism. Their unspoken aim is to rationalize the absence of intellect in modern thought, converting a mere deficiency into a supposed new kind of wisdom. This is to exclude the spiritual capacity of the intelligence and to ensure that its capacity for flight never gets off ground level, so to speak. The dogmatically held belief that human beings, for all their reasoning power, are subject by nature to the same cosmic entanglement as are the animals, has the power of the self-fulfilling prophecy, in that it gives rise to the way of life which exemplifies this condition. For this reason, it can pass almost unchallenged in a world where failure to realize one's spiritual possibilities is almost a norm. Thinkers must speak the language of their time, of course, but what they say must still come from something deeper than the willingness of the public to accept it, or the mission of philosophy will be lost.

ANTI-SPIRITUAL ASSUMPTIONS

In such a mental atmosphere, the most general assumption is that the pursuit of wisdom can only be a matter of taste, that is, of private idiosyncrasy, and not part of our vocation as human beings; and for this reason there is a need for an account of its relevance for everyone. Two other false assumptions related to the above are firstly that we can, if we wish, live without seeking to know; and secondly that the value of what we gain knowledge of results only from either its use as information or from its originality, i.e., an absence of previous claims to have ascertained it.

The first of these two seems justified in view of the limitations imposed on our options by the practical side of life, but only as long as we think of the pursuit of knowledge as a profession. When we consider the conditions of human life more closely, its dynamics are always inseparable from a seeking-to-know, even if it is concerned only with what can be gathered with the eyes and the ears. The seeking of knowledge by one means or another is in fact an activity as continuous as breathing. No matter what we propose as our main occupations, they are nearly always things which would be of no avail without the continual assimilation of knowledge in various ways.

This is a conclusion reached by Aristotle, which he sums up by his maxim that man by his very nature desires to know. For those who prefer to approach this subject from the physical direction, it can be seen that methods of interrogation which involve sensory deprivation confirm in a literally overpowering manner the necessity for a

continual intake of knowledge of one kind or another. Any pro-
longed interruption of it produces unbearable stress, as if to show
that Aristotle's maxim was rather an understatement.

However, the purpose of this argument might possibly be re-
versed if everything, including social life and all leisure pursuits,
imply the absorption of knowledge; if the process is so universal,
why be particular about the forms taken by it? It is true that a minimal psychological equilibrium is satisfied by knowledge gathered
solely at the sensory level as though nothing more was needed.

This non-intellectual approach is bound to pursue knowledge in
endless different directions, none of which is ever followed very far,
gathering things which are too diverse to be able to form a coherent
whole. This option satisfies the purely subjective need for knowledge, but this only shows that the basic needs of sanity are too easily
satisfied in the short-term, in ways that reveal nothing about the
purpose of sanity itself.

Since we always find time for superfluous uses of thought, if only
in fantasy, the intellectualization of thought need not mean an
additional burden so much as a necessary counterpoise to an aimless
use of the mind which would make self-realization impossible.
Attempts to evade this in the name of practicality are really attempts
to enforce a preference for forms of knowledge which can only
crowd out those which could lead to self-knowledge, rather as the
suppression of genuine commerce gives rise to a black market. But
since the pursuit of knowledge is not an option, the only question is
whether it will be creative and free, or whether it will be random,
unfree, and ultimately self-defeating.

The second assumption referred to, that the value of knowledge
depends on its originality, is a common misconception that undermines intellectuality by making one unable to believe in the value of
what one is undertaking. If what one is doing is believed to be just a
rather unnecessary rediscovering of what is well known already, the
essential purpose of discovery will be ignored. The very idea of originality in this realm results from purely human and social considerations like the need to compete for a position in a profession. Here,
the mind is conceived as a tool in the service of temporally arranged
activities, as though it had no meaning or purpose of its own.

But if we only transfer our attention from the outside world long enough to focus on the function of discovery or creative realization as it is in itself, it can be seen that its function is always the same and has the same spiritual power for the individual, regardless of the number of times it may or may not have been experienced by other persons. Even where it appears that a given insight really is original, this may be owing only to our ignorance of the past, since negative conclusions of the kind that no one has ever made this discovery before are notoriously unprovable.

Consequently, the distinction between the re-realization of truths and their official historical origins is as relative as can be on the spiritual level, and another reason for this is that the operation of the intelligence is authentic and 'original' by definition, since knowledge as such must be unmediated. In comparison with this, the distinction between historically original and non-original can be seen for the irrelevance it is, with its fixation on claiming professional and social rewards, and its indifference to the spiritual evolution of the discoverer.

Even though the discovery or rediscovery of a given truth is made easier and more certain for those who follow the original discoverer, its essential function in the soul is still the same. Theoretical insights inevitably react upon self-knowledge, as the properties of the known imply corresponding properties in the knower. The exactitude, immutability, necessity, and universality of the known are a disclosure of the mind's own nature, the discovery of which is perforce original to itself.

INTELLECT AND RELIGIOUS IDEALS

The separation of reason from intellect limits the psychical energies to the outside world and deprives them of their ability to transform the spiritual level of human lives. Far from being another variety of self-aggrandizement, the pursuit of truth rectifies the natural disorders of human nature in a way which transcends the limitations of the ego, not least where its presence is not recognized, because it redeems the solely personal life from its egotism and releases it into the transpersonal and universal.

From a moral point of view, the choice of the intellectual life as a vocation to the extent of one's resources is a pursuit of the ideal which is free from many of the practical limitations which arise in the realm of ideals, whether it is materially rewarding or not. On the other hand, the ideals which are popularly acknowledged today rest more on aspiration than on the chances of actual achievement, as far as the majority are concerned. The improvement of the outside world by direct social and political action is as impossible in any substantial way for most people as the production of great art.

In contrast to this, what the intellectual way requires is in principle possible in its fullness for almost anyone, given only the basics of sincerity and love of truth, and a certain amount of leisure. It therefore has a message and a call for all mankind, no matter how few actually heed it, and it is less impeded by practical obstacles than any other form of the ideal. A world in which its call was heeded to some degree by everyone would be perfectly feasible, and would not disrupt the necessary order of the world. Conversely, this order would certainly be destroyed if every one wanted to engage in the same activity on the practical level.

If there ever was a widespread conversion to truth as a vocation, most of the problems of society would solve themselves, since it would remove the basic evil of aimlessness. It was for this reason that Pascal said that the whole calamity of mankind was owing to the fact that a man cannot remain quietly in one room for any good purpose. Why such a spirituality for Everyman should be ignored in a supposedly democratic age is something of a mystery. Other ideals, whose realization is possible only for members of institutions or small minorities with special talents, way of life and social connections are at bottom socially divisive, since they can only reduce the majority to an audience for the favoured few. Besides, there are various examples of sainthood and of heroism which the great majority have no more chance of imitating than they have of imitating world statesmen.

The implications of this are paradoxical for a morality which tends to see pride in the intellectual way and favour supposedly humbler and more practical paths to perfection. This applies all the more so as the pursuit of truth is still a religious obligation in

Christian tradition, while society professes a passion for sincerity and authenticity. One of the reasons why the intellectual life is so largely ignored as a way of living the ideal may be that many non-imitable examples of excellence are admired because of the fact that they are not practically imitable, not in spite of it. Where there is such a desire for an example which one can approve of with self approval without being personally challenged by it, the problem is inevitably that of sincerity. When we ignore or decline the pursuit of truth as a practical ideal, we need to consider whether we know that we are doing something more important with the available time. Those who can answer this in the affirmative may not be vary numerous, and a great deal of supposed innocence would be compromised as a result.

Another aspect of the pursuit of truth is that one must needs be a moral being while being engaged in it, or it would quickly turn into something else. For this reason it has been described as the only really unselfish activity which is available for most people most of the time.[1] In more religious language, the difference between the intellectual way and the purely moral ones is that the former is opposed to sin by its very nature, while the latter are so only in an extrinsic manner. For the present purpose, we are accepting the usual distinction between pursuit of truth and doing good, but they will be shown in later chapters to have much common ground.

Besides being unselfish, the pursuit of truth as a life goal is an *existentially authentic* option, and one which is largely independent of society. Modern literature is filled with persons who are mysteriously blind to this truth, and therefore try to be authentic persons by almost any means except those which could serve most directly. No doubt this reflects the extent to which modern people suffer from self-hatred, and because of this condition, the ideals of religions become distorted to accommodate those who identify the self as a part of the realm of the trivial and the morally corrupt.

If it is doubted whether a maximum expansion of the moral, intellectual, and creative capacities together could really be God's will for nearly everyone, we need only consider that no one doubts that it is

1. J. Needleman, *The Heart of Philosophy*, Conclusion, pp 234–235.

God's will that human beings should develop from babies into adults. What is involved here is essentially the same process, differing only in degree. The intellectual capacities grow out of the rational soul as naturally as the fruit grows on a tree, and as Providence wills the existence of fruit trees, it must needs will what they produce.

An inability to derive any spiritual benefit from one's output of mental energy is like the absurdity of starving in the midst of plenty. Some such perception as this may have prompted Blake's 'To the Christians.' The fact that it is part of a poetical vision means that it deserves to carry so much the more weight, and in any case it is both an apt conclusion to this chapter and an introduction to the next:

> I know of no other Christianity and no other Gospel than the liberty of both body and mind to exercise the Divine Arts of Imagination. Imagination, the real and eternal world of which this Vegetable Universe is but a faint shadow, and in which we shall live in our Eternal or Imaginative Bodies when these Vegetable Mortal Bodies are no more. The Apostles knew of no other Gospel. What are all their spiritual gifts? What is the Divine Spirit? Is the Holy Ghost any other than an intellectual fountain? What is the harvest of the Gospel and its labours? What is that talent which it is a curse to hide?[2]

Taken too literally, this might seem to say that religion and culture were the same thing, but in fact it means that the living out of the truth must include its intellective possibilities among the others. In revealed religion, man is addressed from above the level of the intellect, not to displace it, but to raise it to its proper place in the person and in the world.

2. William Blake, *Jerusalem*, 77.

5

CREATIVITY
AND SPIRITUALITY

THE ANOMALY OF CREATIVITY

What has been said about the intellectual or contemplative way and its spiritual potentialities can be extended to the realm of creativity. The difference is not absolute because all acts of insight are implicitly creative, though the creative can be pursued for its own sake, even to the extent of making one uncritical of the sources of one's inspiration. But despite its close affinity with the contemplative life, religious and mystical authors have little or nothing to say about the part it can play in regard to their ideals. As a result, it is usually seen as a secular occupation which participates in the sacred only in a more or less accidental or inessential manner. However, it is too deeply rooted in the use of free will and the love of truth for this to be justified in principle, as will appear from an examination of its deeper meaning.

In all forms of creativity, the free will is active in a special manner, since one is not moved by externals but by universal values seen with 'the eye of the soul.' Its relation to freedom appears where the production of something new and original cannot be seen to be connected by natural causes to what went before it. Must there not have been an intervention from some source outside the flow of natural forces with their cycle of stimulus and response? It certainly appears that the achievements of creative inspiration are an extension of our metaphysical freedom. The relation between creativity and free will is specially important for full personhood, as is shown by the difficulty which even free will alone presents to metaphysical systems which exclude personality. Spontaneity above all, whether it appears in some morally inspired action or in a work of art, is an insuperable problem for monistic systems which aim at a totalitarian comprehensiveness, and the problem is only aggravated by the fact that these systems themselves are demonstrably products of creative spontaneity.

AN ARCHETYPAL VIEW OF CREATION

Those who would deny the reality of creativity argue that man cannot really create anything, but can only make new combinations of things which have always existed. But while this is true in the trite sense that we cannot bring things out of nothing, there is no need to confine the question to absolute creation. The discovery and expression of hitherto unknown relationships among preexistent realities is still a production of something out of nothing in a relative sense, which is nonetheless real. If the art or field of endeavour in question is conceived as being made up of Forms or Archetypes, the finished result of the creative process would be the instancing of another such archetypal reality which had not been manifest in the outside world. In the creative act itself, this final result had become visible to the mind's eye of the human agent who subsequently captured it in the appropriate medium, being guided by a grasp of intelligible realities and not by anything available to the senses. Once this has been achieved, there is no limit to the ways in which contemplation of this work by others can enable them to reproduce for themselves the original vision of the creative mind. What was once a flash of insight may then become part of a language or of a way of life.

There is thus a certain discontinuity between man's relative creation and the natural conditions on which it was based, and the greater the creative genius involved, the greater the discontinuity. But the problem here is that the scope of this idea is much wider than the realm of the morally good, since it could just as well include the devising of the perfect crime as well as the production of a thing of beauty, and this is what accounts for the suspicion with which creativity as a value is often regarded. Many such achievements are just morally and even aesthetically neutral, as with technological inventions which are nevertheless also products of the 'poetic' principle in the broadest sense of the word. This in itself would bring us back to the commonplace idea that the decisive factor must be the intentions with which this kind of work is undertaken, and thence to the equally commonplace conclusion that its value comes from the intentions and not from the creativity itself.

However, it is not true to say that the creative act cannot have an intrinsic merit just because that merit is not unconditional. For those who misunderstand this, the production of a work of art and the digging of a ditch would be alike in being forms of work, worldly activities requiring a certain amount of energy, and so spiritually on the same level. Their merits would in either case be relative only to the intentions with which they were executed. The mistake here is to make no distinction between the creative act and its products.

This perspective of conventional morality is only right insofar as moral intention does affect the value of creativity, but wrong in thinking that that gives it all its value, as it does with simple labour. Rather it is the case that a harmony with moral value serves to liberate the intrinsic merit of the creative, realizing something beyond moral intention alone. This is what can overcome the objection that creativity can serve evil as easily as good. Besides, the fact that it is intrinsically allied to the good is shown by the fact that it is above all an application of free will. Just as the essential value of free will is not diminished by the fact that we can choose wrong as well as right, the issue is no different with regard to creativity.

There is, however, an obvious difference as well in that free will is to some degree exercised by all, whereas creativity in its most sophisticated forms is of interest only to certain minorities. This is another reason why orthodox religion disregards its merits, though this can only be justified by reasons of expediency. To confine free will solely to moral action would border on utilitarianism.

The limitation of being a specialized concern for a small minority applies only to its most abstruse productions, and such objections to it are more than offset by the way in which it discloses something essential to the human state itself. For this reason, it is not hard to maintain that cultural 'creation' is a valid analogue in the human microcosm of the Divine *fiat lux* in the universe.

CREATIVITY RESISTANT TO SYSTEMS

Creativity presents a problem for all systematic conceptions of reality, whether they are religious, scientific, philosophical, or mystical. While it is not remarkable that creativity is not linked with grace in exoteric religion, for the reasons just outlined, it is surprising that the problem it raises exists in an aggravated form for the more mystical and esoteric forms of religion. In the latter, it would seem natural to expect that ways would be found to unify the creative and spiritual dimensions. But in reality, metaphysical religion, for all its soaring flights of intuition, is no more equal to this purpose than is the most narrowly conceived orthodoxy. The reason for this is that when things are known, they are in a sense frozen, since they cannot then be other than what they are, and this gives rise to a critical problem when one claims universal knowledge. Creative free will is an instantaneous act which cannot be grasped in this way, and esoteric systems which ignore this end up with a falsely simplified idea of reality which has clear parallels with that of physical science. But their conclusions differ from those of science in that they typically assume that the knower can somehow become absorbed into their 'frozen' concept of total reality, not just in a mental way, but in an ontological way as well.

The final goal of such thought would seem to be a clear, bright, homogeneous world in which the knower is eliminated and the truth somehow knows itself without the complications of innumerable minds relating to it and reflecting it independently. Still less can such a conception allow any room for free will or creative action. A reality which was in effect one great theorem contemplating its own proof would imply that ultimate reality must be an immobile abstraction. By a strange kind of irony, this kind of ideal merges with what was identified in chapter 2 as the basic condition for sin.

The supposed ideal perfection of such world-systems always stumbles against the fact that they are productions of the creative inspiration of individuals, who remain transcendent, even in relation to the highest conceptions they are able to formulate; the latter are necessarily in them, and not vice-versa. Eyesight reflects this fact in its own way, where it takes in everything except the perceiving organ itself.

The pantheistic system which has no room for the free creative act is even more closed in this respect than is theistic religion with its belief in personality. Given the idea of real personality, the soul has by nature a privileged position in relation to theorems and Forms, almost as much as in relation to physical objects, for the reasons given before. Though systems can express major truths, their intrinsic limit lies in the freedom of knowers to know them, which is a reality they cannot contain. Their denial of freedom is thus a paradox which, qua systems, they are not able to resolve.

If the knower cannot equate himself with the known in the realm of ideas without a denial of the difference between the soul and its represented objects, no more will he be able to do this on the material level, as evolutionist thought supposes from its own point of view. As it bases everything on the material level, it is to that extent the very opposite of the mystical position just referred to. Nevertheless, it excludes the creative principle on a physical basis just as much as the other does on the metaphysical. In either case, what is missing is something analogous to the free space used by our limbs when they have work to do, or to the peace and quiet necessary for concentration and mental tasks. This would amount to a void or non-being, enclosing both the knower and the known, allowing the knower to relate to things knowable in countless different combinations and proportions. Such metaphysical space may appear to be negative purely and simply, and yet for all that, it comprises something without which the positive realities of wisdom and theory would be as inoperative as things in a museum. The same idea is expressed by Lao Tzu as follows:

> *Thirty spokes will converge*
> *In the hub of a wheel;*
> *But the use of the cart*
> *Will depend on the part of the hub that is void.*[1]

---

1. Lao Tzu, *Tao Te Ching*, chap. 11, Blackney translation.

The resolution of the problem as to what is necessary for freedom and creativity may be found on a basis suggested by this Taoist teaching. This would bring the Yin-Yang concept into the Theory of Forms. The Forms are nearly always conceived in terms of the 'Yang' side of the issue, that is, as positive values above all else. However, this need not exclude the hollow, passive, and silent parts of reality from being true realities in their own way. Were it otherwise, there would be no means whereby mutually compatible Forms could make combinations, nor could there be any means by which our minds could relate to the Forms in order to know them. For this reason, Plato argues that the realm of Forms must contain its own equivalent of motion, and therefore of space itself as well:

> If knowing is to be acting on something, it follows that what is known must be acted upon by it; and so, on this showing, Reality when it is being known by the act of knowledge must, insofar as it is known, be changed owing to being so acted upon ... are we really to be so easily convinced that change, life, soul, understanding have no place in that which is perfectly real—that it has neither life nor thought, but stands immutable in solemn aloofness, devoid of intelligence? ... In that case we must admit that what changes and change itself are real things. The philosopher must refuse to accept from the champions either of the One or of the many Forms the doctrine that all reality is changeless; and he must turn a deaf ear to the other party who represent Reality as everywhere changing. Like a child begging for 'both', he must declare that Reality, or the sum of things, is both at once—all that is unchangeable and all that is in change.[2]

Despite the appearance of paradox, therefore, it is consistent with the Theory of Forms to include therein negative or 'Yin' Forms, that is empty possibilities among the eternal realities. To make the real consist exclusively of the positive Forms would eliminate all activity, and therefore knowledge itself. Without the void, there could be only one real being, and one which could not even know itself. Given only the unchanging, we are assured of the content of knowledge while

---

2. Plato, *Sophist*, 248E–249D.

being denied any means of obtaining it. Conversely, with universal flux theories, we are allowed the investigative and creative activities, while there are no abiding realities for our statements to be true about. Therefore both knowledge and creativity require that the ultimate realities should include Forms of motion, and by implication, Forms of unfilled possibilities. The presence of the latter Forms would overcome the monolithic and deterministic character which this metaphysic can sometimes assume, besides removing a theoretical objection to the soul's creative freedom in relation to the archetypal realities and their interrelationships.

CONFORMING TO THE DIVINE PATTERN

This modification to the Theory of Forms, with its implications for the soul's moral freedom, removes grounds for conflict between it and Christian doctrine. While everything produced by natural causes is explicable in terms of its physical antecedents, creative and morally free acts mingle elements drawn directly from the Forms with the flow of natural causality. Closely connected with this is the Christian discovery of the reality of personality which implies an individual agency which is much more than the simply physical kind.

To further confirm the spiritual status of creativity, it can be put in relation to orthodoxy as follows. The monotheistic religions conceive of God as the Creator of the world, while in the moral sphere, they make it a duty for man to become God-like by learning to share in the Divine nature. If these values are set down in a kind of syllogism, their implication will be clearer:

(1) God is understood as the Creator;
(2) Man's duty is to become as much like God as possible;
(3) Those who live creatively are fulfilling the second requirement in a specially direct manner.

The only restriction that need be applied to this conclusion is 'other things being equal,' in accordance with what was said earlier in connection with moral values, because creativity cannot be assumed to be a merit in the absence of the more universal values which are necessary for all mankind and all vocations. But given a foundation in the kind of merit which is an issue for everyone, the conclusion as to creativity is undeniable. However, there remains the difficulty that it is not enjoined by any positive commandment in Scripture.

One answer to this would be that such a commandment would conflict with the spontaneity necessary for creativity, besides which, a commandment must by definition apply directly to everyone. The force of a commandment comes from the fact that it expresses a norm below which no one should fall, and not from its requiring something of a special nature. In this connection, Berdyaev states that:

> human creativity is not a claim or a right on the part of man, but God's claim on, and call to man. God awaits man's creative act, which is the response to the creative act of God. What is true of man's freedom is true also of his creativity, for freedom too is God's summons to man and man's duty to God. God does not reveal to man that which it is for man to reveal to God. Man awaits the birth of God in himself and God awaits the birth of man in himself.[3]

The impossibility of our revealing anything in an absolute sense to an omniscient being should not prevent our seeing that Divine revelation implies a countermovement from man which has the form of a revelation from the human to the Divine. Divine revelation therefore prompts two kinds of response, which should not exclude one another: (a) that of accepting and propagating revelation more or less as it came to oneself, and (b) that of responding with a counter-revelation which is informed by values and principles which are latent in the original.

However, Berdyaev's bold conception of creative action provokes the question as to whether God could really need anything from us in the form of creativity or intellectuality. The common sense and conventional religious answer is, of course not. It must be a contradiction to say that the Creator needed anything from His own creatures. Nothing more could be said as long as the word 'need' is

---

3. N. Berdyaev, *Dream and Reality*, chap. 8, pp 208–209.

understood only in the basic sense in which we need food and shelter. However, a very different answer is possible here, one which hardly ever seems to be noticed. There can be such a thing as a self-imposed need, or a 'free necessity', which must be possible for God as much as for man.

For example, a wealthy benefactor who gives a town a public library becomes thereby in need of the people to be readers of the books in it. Though he needed nothing from them, he can create a certain need by his own choice. Similarly, if God bestows intellective and creative capacities on human beings, He can thereby be said to create a self-imposed need for the things which those capacities can achieve. A need of this kind is clearly compatible with omnipotence, so that there is a real sense in which human powers in this realm can supply Divine needs. The secularization of creativity, and its separation from the last ends of life can obscure this spiritual dimension, but cannot eradicate or devalue it.

6

'HAPPINESS AND THE EXTENSION OF TIME'

HAPPINESS DISTINCT FROM PLEASURE

The title of this chapter is that of the fifth tractate of the first of the Enneads, and it concerns something vital to the understanding of life's purpose, something which must be understood if we are to grasp the reasonable aspect of moral codes which may seem inhumanly demanding, or at least arbitrary. Part of the problem involved here is that human nature is reluctant to observe the distinction between happiness and pleasure. But not only are they distinct, they are to a large extent separable, and even, up to a point, in conflict. A life which is lived on the assumption that they can be treated as though they were the same thing will never be able to realize its own meaning and purpose.

The key to this issue involves an idea which has personal relevance and which can be grasped as a theoretical certainty. It appears in a text of Plotinus which is of metaphysical and psychological importance at the same time, and concerns states of pleasure and pain in regard to the passage of time, and all forms of acquisition which may be pleasurable or painful:

> If in the greater length of time a man has seen more deeply, time has certainly done something for him, but if all the process has brought him no further vision, then one glance would give all he has had.... In the matter of sorrows and pains there is, no doubt, ground for saying that time brings increase, for example in a lingering malady, but if the constitution did not deteriorate,

if the mischief grew no worse, then here too, there would be no trouble but that of the present moment.[1]

The only medium in which pleasurable or painful states can accrue to us is that of time, whence it follows that the ways in which our experiences of them relate to one another cannot differ from the ways in which their respective parts of time are related. Although what follows from this will seem opposed to common sense, this is only because of an habitual failure to discriminate between the content of experiences and the way in which these experiences relate to one another.

The basic prejudice of common sense in this sphere is that the repetition of any experience, good or bad, adds to the total amount of either which one has obtained, a total which grows in proportion to the number of repetitions. One kind of pleasure or pain repeated on ten occasions must mean ten times the pleasure or pain of any one of them. This is one of man's most deeply-rooted assumptions, and is responsible for the other assumption that happiness must result from an accumulation of pleasures. It is nevertheless nothing but an illusion, even though it is strong enough to persist even when its deception has been explained.

The essential reason why the good or ill of two days is not in reality double that of one of them lies in the undeniable property of time that each of its successive moments is in effect a separate world for experience. Like Leibniz' 'windowless' monads, the moment neither receives anything from, nor imparts anything to, any other moment, not even to the next ones adjacent to it. Here is the basis of the fact that what is once past, be it only by a moment, is as much beyond our grasp as the remotest antiquity This property of temporal moments, and therefore of their contents as well, which could rightly be called atomic, does not allow the least possibility that any of them could be combined to make a total in this world, while we live in time and matter. Even though moments may be permanent in higher dimensions, that could not enlarge the content of any one of them.

---

1. *Enneads*, I, 5, 3 and I, 5, 6.

For this reason, one cannot challenge the truism that the pleasures of today can get no supplement from those of yesterday, and this carries the further implication that the greatest amount of pleasure of whatever kind can never exceed the greatest single instance of it, and likewise with pain. All the other instances of the same kind of pleasure or pain do no more than approach more or less closely the maximal amount, only to revert each time to the same starting point as before, according as the contents of their respective moments fall short of the maximal case.

Where repetition or continuation seem to make pleasures or pains increase, this results solely from changes in our constitution or our sensibility, and not from the repetition as such. In relation to any actual present moment, all previous moments are effectively non-existent, and for this reason Plotinus says that:

> to make multiplicity, whether in time or in action, essential to happiness, is to put it (happiness) together *by combining non-existents*, represented by the past, with some one thing that actually is.[2]

Thus our near-instinctive belief that our total good is augmented by the repetition of anything related to it is in reality so irrational that the only adequate comparisons are such as could not be taken seriously. For example, a supposed belief that one could get progressively nearer to a given destination the more often one goes half way there, turns back and starts again. The futility of the latter case can easily be seen because there are no emotive causes conflicting with the ability to see it, but the principle is the same as with the repetition-illusion.

IMPLICATIONS FOR ASCETIC VALUES

Nothing could be more important for real happiness than to dissipate the psychological force of the repetition-illusion by recalling the facts about time and the temporal condition which show its

---

2. *Enneads*, I, 5, 10.

falsehood. Without this, all attempts at wisdom are bound to prove as ineffectual as baking with sand instead of dough, as in the Buddhist simile. At best, such wisdom would only be an abstract knowledge of principles with no power over one's essential being. The self-understanding involved here transforms the commonplace options of pursuit of pleasure and its avoidance. The ascetic denial of pleasure, if misunderstood, can remain as much trapped in the common sense attitude to temporality as is the worldly belief in pleasure. In this case, its good intentions are not matched by objective knowledge, and one fails to see that what is really being discarded is only an imaginary good which is not part of the good of the here and now. Similarly, the prolongation of unpleasant states will cause less distress once it is understood that the real evil is not actually increased by the number of instances of it, no matter what effect they may have on the imagination.

Another result is that we are now in a position to get free from the modern inability to understand the ascetic ideals and way of life which are to be found in nearly all ages and cultures except the present one. Part of the purpose of ascetic practices is to liberate the mind and will from their bondage to temporality and repetition in a practical rather than a theoretical manner. In this way, one's relation to God can become real and not just theoretical. Once the truth about the temporal condition is understood, there is no problem in understanding the severe measures that have always been used to attack the roots of our illusion, and one's judgement as to how much is really lost in the ascetically-limited life will be altered fundamentally. The widespread confusion between self-denial and self-punishment can easily be resolved, which is the more necessary today, when religious belief alone does not free one from this confusion.

The affliction of modern humanity is not so much an addiction to pleasure as a mental enslavement to time and temporality, as the former is a symptom of the latter. This condition has developed something like an instinct for avoidance of the external limitations which could foster the sense of eternity without which aspirations to spirituality must be mere dreams, or at best hopeful desires. The natural desire to live as long as possible can only be rational on condition that one is continuing to advance further into the ideal. The loss of life is by definition the loss of the state comprised in the present moment which is equally great and equally small in the oldest person as in the youngest. The more ignorant we are about the temporal condition the more we shall fear death. Nearly all passions, including fear, greed and lust, result from an avid grasp at a life whose real nature is not understood.

COLLECTIVE SUFFERING

The examination of the temporal condition made here has a significant parallel where the pleasures and pains of large numbers of persons are concerned. The same principle operates in such cases. If we hear of one person killed in an accident, we may not take much notice of it, but if we hear of dozens of persons killed, the natural feeling is that the evil must be much greater. But in reality there is no mind and no organism experiencing the pains or deaths of dozens of persons. The maximum distress is always neither more nor less than that of one victim. In this example, the sufferings of many different persons are the analogue of the experiences contained in the separate moments of one person's life. In neither case is there any place in which the experiences *per se* can be made into any objective total or larger entity. This is not to say that long experience cannot enrich a personality with memories and deepening insight, but this results from a progressive modification of the soul by means of its own relations to its contents, and not by any substantive total of these contents.

Connected with this is the surprising fact that physical pleasures and pains do not actually leave any trace on the memory. If it should appear that they do, closer examination will show that what is really remembered is only the circumstances of the pain or pleasure, not the thing itself. One reason why memories tend to be enhanced with the passage of time is just because the elements of physical distress are lost before anything else.

So much of life consists in repetitions, which is necessary up to a point, since it is only through repetition that we can learn how to classify and identify things, but the real difference made by the above analysis does not lie in denying activity so much as in ridding it of its poison. If we were to go out of our way to avoid action on the grounds that temporal processes do not realize totals, we should be just as deluded as if we believed in such summations, for if it is foolish to pursue a mirage it must be equally foolish to flee from it. By concentration on the real and objective good we can awaken from the time-bound dream which spoils natural and spiritual life equally.

7

TRANSCENDENCE
AND NORMAL EXPERIENCE

THE INNER DUALITY OF CONSCIOUSNESS

The transcendent dimension of everyday consciousness is evidenced by unmistakable signs if one knows how to look for them. Far from needing the extraordinary experiences of a mystic, an analysis of what is well known already will suffice for this purpose. This runs counter to the impression made by life's pressures, conflicts and pains, which seem to form an insurmountable obstacle to higher states of consciousness by binding one to a stream of events which we think have no relation to it. Nevertheless, it can be shown that an effectual contact with the transcendent is present even in experiences which most seem to contradict it, and the essential insight in this regard is again indicated by Plotinus where he uses the sensation of distress to argue that at a deeper level the soul is always unmoved, comparing its awareness to the message brought by a messenger:

> We cannot describe the perception itself as distress; it is the knowledge of the distress and, being knowledge, is not itself affected, or it could not know and convey a true message: a messenger, affected, overwhelmed by the event, would either not convey the message or not convey it very faithfully.[1]

Here, in the midst of the most ordinary experience we have the far-reaching principle that the truthful grasp of even the strongest

1. *Enneads* IV, 4, 19.

impression depends as much on the core of our consciousness remaining unaffected by it as upon the cause of the event in question. Otherwise, we should be left with the paradox that, if our entire being were pervaded by its physical and emotional reactions, this very state would subvert our means of knowing that we were in any such state at all. It could be objected that this is to assume that our self-awareness is indeed objective and truthful. What if some impressions did prevent the transmission of awareness? Would we ever know? There has to be some distinction between consciousness and its contents, but this may not mean that we have to claim so much for consciousness as an independent reality. However, what is involved here depends on a strict polarity between what in us is 'moved' and what is not, these two being bound together by a kind of mutual dependence. Kant expressed this relationship as follows: 'For it is this very notion of the permanent which renders possible the representation of a transition from one state to another,' and he says that the changes which lead from non-being to being have to be conceived 'as alternating determinations of that which is permanent.' [2]

All experience involves a fundamental duality, this time between what could be called the 'inner' and 'outer' functions of experience. Although these two are always joined, it is not hard to separate them conceptually. This duality is not the same as that of the outside world itself and our representation of it, which was discussed in Chapter 1. Unlike the latter, this is not a duality between two classes of phenomena, but a duality between two dimensions of the consciousness which forms the representations.

THE CORE OF CONSCIOUSNESS

Because of the essentially transcendent part of consciousness, an absolutely evil state of being would be a self-contradiction, which shows the essentially parasitic nature of evil, since nothing bad can begin to exist unless there is first something good to be corrupted.

2. Kant, *Critique of Pure Reason*, 'The Permanence of Substance'.

The general principle involved here leads to a number of developments in which parallel conclusions apply to particular evils such as injustice, futility, and deception.

This can be seen to be an extension of what was said in chapter 2, where we considered the center of consciousness which was beyond the reach of the deceptions from which the outer man suffers. In a similar way, Augustine taught that in every rational soul there is a core of certainties which is independent of sensory experience. The more our experiences in the outside world clash with these native certainties, the more we are made aware of their presence in us, and hence the feeling of conflict. For example, a negation like injustice awakens the awareness of a justice which is an intrinsic principle both in the mind and in the world-order. The implications of this are important both theoretically and practically, since they give answers to doubts as to whether philosophy can really transcend the disorders of natural existence and effectively contact their invisible origin.

The same idea is expressed by C.S. Lewis in connection with the waste, cruelty and purposelessness we see in the universe. These things, he states, can only be identified as 'real evils' if their contraries are somehow preestablished as a law pervading all things:

> Unless we judge this waste and cruelty to be real evils, we cannot of course condemn the universe for exhibiting them. Unless we take our own standard of goodness to be valid in principle (however fallible our particular applications of it), we cannot mean anything by calling waste and cruelty evils. And unless we take our own standard to be *something more than ours*, to be in fact an objective principle to which we are responding, we cannot regard that standard as valid. In a word, unless we allow ultimate reality to be moral, we cannot morally condemn it.[3]

Thus consciousness of the evils which would negate the essential values would not be possible unless those values remained unmoved in the mind, in the face of all opposing impressions. These values belong to the intellect and so are not governed by the emotive,

3. C.S. Lewis, *Christian Reflections*, 'De Futilitate'.

imaginary, and sentient functions of the soul, and for this reason they cannot create any subjective clamor in their own interests like the other faculties. The Forms of the intellect can only assert their reality in indirect ways, and not surprisingly they are generally ignored as far as possible in a materialistic culture, for which the True and the Good are deemed to consist only of things which most people believe they want, and never anything not subject to the will.

The contemplative way has an aspect of emptiness, even though it is only an emptiness at the sensory and egotistical level, whereas it has both fullness and activity on its own level. Conversely, the widespread inability to rise above the world of objects, for all its apparent activity, reveals a passivity at the deepest level. But however much it may be ignored, the intellect with its universal norms remains part of the archetypal Form of the human state, so that its reemergence after times of oblivion is always inevitable.

THEOLOGY AND REDUCTIONISM

The above property of the intellect underlies what was said previously about its belonging to both the natural and the supernatural at the same time, and so not being bound by the conventional frontiers between the divine and the human. The fact that the natural and the supernatural are separate objective realities does not imply a corresponding objectivity for the boundaries set up between them. The ambivalence of the intellect in this regard serves only to increase the resistance to its point of view by modern thought, because the latter is dominated by specialization. Thus, for example, there is a fortuitous alignment on an academic level between the positions of modern philosophy and theology, because neither feels any need for a conception which combines transcendence and logic, the one not wanting the intelligence to have a spiritual dimension, and the other not wanting an approach to God which was not part of historical revelation. Nevertheless, this creation of islands of specialized activity flies in the face of the living continuum of reality which is not ruled by man-made barriers.

The practical excuse for the theological side of this issue is that things are always weighted in favor of the merely natural condition by a kind of spiritual law of gravity. Consequently, reliance on intellect alone can easily lead to a descent into ordinary life and a fading of vision. The role of intellect may be independent of symbol and sacrament in theory, but in practice it does not prevail unless life at the sense level is subject to a spiritual counter-force on the same level. This is also connected with the fact that the intellect in us cannot call itself into activity, since it is the psychical and personal powers which must resonate with it and allow it to be manifested.

The fact that activity of this kind can come only from the individual part of the self is simply a consequence of the unity of the person, since an autonomous will for the intellect would divide it from the person, and turn it into a separate being. This does not detract from the perfection proper to the intellect because it is not altered in itself by the fact that in man it holds a peripheral position in regard to his being as a whole, and this is a natural consequence of man's lowly place in the spiritual order. Consequently, the dependence of the higher on the lower powers for their expression in the context of human life is no more an argument against intellectual certainty than the need to switch on a lamp could reduce its light.

What has now been said concerning the transcendent element in consciousness can be applied to the doctrine of the Fall, by which it is understood that after a certain time humanity lost its original perfection and became hereditarily subject to sin and mortality from then on. At first sight, this doctrine must appear incompatible with our possession of any transcendental principle by natural right, and this is often taken to be the case. The solution to this riddle is implicit in what has been argued already and it is aptly contained in an aphorism of Frithjof Schuon, that that in us which convinces us we are despicable cannot itself be despised. This is an application to moral values of the Plotinian idea that 'a messenger affected... would either not convey the message or not convey it very faithfully.'

Consequently, it would be self-contradictory to believe oneself to be *wholly* in a fallen state and at the same time to be able to know it for what it is and accept responsibility for it. Taken in full literalness, the Fall would mean that human nature was corrupted in its entirety, a view which Augustine came close to holding, despite the conception of the intrinsic certainties of the intellect which appears in his philosophical works. This strange contradiction may have arisen from a belief that he had to put what was opportune for the needs of most people before systematic consistency.

Were we indeed wholly corrupted, no one would ever have shown the sincerity and goodwill to acknowledge the fact, (the usual determination of present-day society to deny or ignore the Fall is thus an indication of extreme corruption), and possibly no one should even have been able to understand what was meant by the idea. If, then, there were really nothing in us unaffected by the Fall, the words 'I am a sinner' would involve a logical paradox not very different from that of 'I am telling a lie,' But as no one ever believes that faith really implies such a paradox, the only alternative is the 'naturally supernatural' element in our being which has been the subject of this chapter. This could truly judge the part of the self which was corrupted. Besides being further described by Plotinus as a part of the soul which never descends into this world with us, but remains always among the eternals, the same idea was revealed to Julian of Norwich, who expresses it thus:

> In every soul to be saved is a good will that has never consented to sin, in the past or in the future. Just as there is an animal will in our lower nature that does not will what is good, so there is a godly will in our higher part, which by its basic goodness never wills what is evil, but only what is good. . . . [and] We are God's creation twice: essential being and sensual nature. Our being is that higher part which we have in our Father, God almighty, and the Second Person of the Trinity is Mother of this basic nature, since he has taken our sensual nature upon himself.[4]

Here we see clearly distinguished the intellectual center of our being and the personal soul, the latter comprising the 'I' to which we can justly attribute sin and folly; this is what suffers the consequences of the Fall.

---

4. *Revelations of Divine Love*, 37 and 58.

A RADICAL CONCLUSION

By a turn of dialectic, then, it appears that the doctrine of the Fall itself implies the counter idea of something in our nature exempt from it. This can explain the difference made to moral priorities, depending on whether they apply to our ego and its will or whether to the life of consciousness. The latter is supra-individual in principle, so that its merits cannot be reckoned in the same way as those of our specifically individual activities. Its main moral imperative is simply fidelity to its calling, because it has primacy owing to its relation to the transcendent center of consciousness. As such it is the end or goal of all other forms of activity.

This property of contemplative activity has been expressed by Maritain from the point of view that the moral and social virtues are ancillary to the life of the contemplative. This kind of person serves the common good by 'the sole fact that by him human nature attains its end, and that in him the human City produces its noblest fruit.' [5]

This is bound up with the idea of a special category of knowledge which does not serve any ulterior purposes, but is worth knowing solely for its own sake. Those who are most involved with such knowledge would therefore be in their own persons the realization of all the practical purposes which are pursued in the world around them. Such is the real basis for the idea of the superman, which is much more ancient than the non-intellectual travesty of it which was made by Nietzsche. Far from being the negation of morality, the superman is free from some of the practical implications of morality only by identifying with the intelligible source from whence morality arises, more than with many of its practical applications.

Such an alternative to the usual moral options assumes only that the chain of human purposes does not extend to infinity, and that all these purposes exist on an ascending scale of importance. The ideas of involvement and commitment which this possibility gives rise to differ greatly from the publicly-recognized ones in today's society. Such an apparently detached mode of being and acting can

5. J. Maritain, *Theonas: Conversations With a Sage*, 2nd conversation.

appear to be irresponsible and of no use to anyone but oneself, from a utilitarian point of view, at least. Just how mistaken such an impression would be can also be seen from the fact that contemplative activity belongs to the real self as defined before, while specifically practical morality pertains mainly to the ego.

8

THE ABSTRACT
AND THE CONCRETE

COMMON SENSE CONCRETENESS

Since the word 'concrete' is habitually used interchangeably with 'physical', language creates an obstacle to understanding what this idea really involves. So-called concrete realities obviously give something which subtler ones do not, but there is a deception in this which is usually ignored. It may be said in a general way that concrete realities fill our world of representation, and that they are therefore alien to us in their inner essences, for all their power to captivate attention. It is possible to show that the abstract and the concrete are largely misplaced conceptions in popular usage, and in so doing, one of the main objections to belief in metaphysical reality can be removed.

The question as to what is abstract and what is concrete is related to that of the real and the illusory. Any revaluation of the common sense ideas in this regard will call for a deeper conception of the concrete and a loosening of its connection with materiality. Where common sense cannot be endorsed, it will be necessary to find reasons which carry more conviction than does the impression of concreteness which the material world constantly creates.

The main force behind the usual sense of the concrete is apparent in the radical difference between thoughts and things, by which ideas seem insubstantial and not wholly real. As there seems to be no continuity between material things and ideas, there is always the feeling that ideas are somehow phantasmal in relation to the physical world, no matter how much truth is known to reside in them. In merely creating awareness of this deep difference, experience is not deceptive, but it becomes so as soon as one tries to explain it in terms of a lesser reality in thoughts and ideas. Concreteness may well be manifest to many different degrees, but we need to understand why there really are no practical grounds for making full concreteness peculiar to the physical realm.

Two things which particularly appear as evidence for material concreteness are, firstly the comparative lack of change undergone by material things in a given length of time, compared with thoughts; and secondly, the impact of one material thing on another, whether it be a fragile object striking a hard one or the hand's pain on striking a hard object. These impact phenomena have no equivalent in the mental realm, for however contrary two ideas may be they always have a certain impassivity regardless of their degrees of truth or falsity. Ideas are by their very nature individuated independently of the accidents of space, time, and matter.

The implications of this are the exact opposite of what is usually held to be the case, for the impact of one material object upon another results not from the power of these objects but from their lack of it. Whatever part of space a material object occupies, it has to exclude all others from that space, just as they exclude it from theirs. One need only contrast this with ideas' independence of location and their mutual co-extensiveness for it to appear that material things are mutually exclusive because of inertia, opacity, and unqualified finitude, all indicating a lower degree of reality.

Their mutual exclusion does not even bring them any greater degree of individuation, since ideas can exclude one another much more profoundly without any such mechanical attributes. That these objects physically exclude one another leads directly to their most prominent property, namely their mutual destructiveness. Obviously, there could be no other basis on which they could break, crush, grind, or disperse one another, and the dramatic sensory qualities of these effects are taken by common sense as further evidence for the concreteness of the objects concerned.

Nevertheless, the real implication is the exact opposite, since all that is really involved here is the inability of these objects to retain their physical forms or keep more than a temporary foothold on physical existence. Such is the rational conclusion, but it is not by reason that this question is usually judged, but by imagination. Naturally, all destructive processes create vivid sensory images, from whence imagination and memory inevitably pronounce 'more real' whatever is the more productive of such phenomena.

In the realm of mind, on the other hand, it is the power of the subtle realities it contains which gives them a stability and a uniformity which can easily give rise to the negative impression of ineffectuality in contrast to the dynamic aspect of the material realm, where irreversible and startling changes constantly occur.

MEDIATION BY LIVING ORGANISMS

A useful insight into the comparison between intellectual and material realities is given by living organisms. These occupy a position midway between these extremes because, like material things, they are liable to the same kinds of physical accidents or destruction, but unlike the purely material, they have the power of recovering their physical forms if the injury is not too great. In this way, they can be more durable than steel under certain conditions. In this respect, they have some share in the indestructible and self-subsistent realities of intellect. The power of living things to heal themselves and grow anew contradicts the supposition that only material things are fully concrete, for if this were true, the inorganic realm would be the one with the greatest powers of self-preservation and self-renewal.

On the contrary, living organisms, *qua* living, demonstrate an essentially stronger hold on existence which is not affected by how long they remain alive, and their participation in the mental and intellective orders leaves little doubt as to the source of their superiority in this regard. Starting at the limits of the inorganic realm, and ascending from the lowest forms of life to the highest, it can be seen that the presence of the material component has as much and as little importance at either extreme, since the advance in complexity comes not from the addition of matter but from the degree of organization brought into it by something which is not material. The living organism also continues to exist by means of its activity, whereas the continuation of inorganic existence is simply a result of inertia.

It may be asked whether the destructive and dramatic impacts of the material things may not indicate some other kind of concreteness in the objects concerned. But despite their appeal to the imagination, such tests of concreteness cannot be valid tests, not only because they depend on the inertia just referred to, but more especially because no criterion can form a part of the things that it is used to judge. In other words, if a material object gives the impression of concreteness only in relation to other material objects, this could no more prove its concreteness than a collision of two objects in a dream could prove theirs. The whole apparent power and concreteness of material things results from the fact, expressed in Thomas Taylor's translation of Plotinus, that 'debility is valid against debility.'

The size of the paradox is not understated:

> But body, a non-existence? Mountain and rock, the wide solid earth, all that exists, all that can be struck and driven, surely all proclaims the real existence of the corporeal? And how, it will be asked can we, on the contrary, attribute Being, and the only Authentic Being, to entities like Soul and Intellect, things having no weight or pressure, yielding to no force, offering no resistance, things not even visible? ... Things whose nature represents a diminishment have no power of recuperation ... thus what has most definitely become body, having most closely approximated to non-being, lacks the strength to re-knit its unity: the heavy and violent crash of body against body works destruction, and weak is powerful against weak, non-being against its like.[1]

As purely material things have too little power to conserve their being, except when they are undisturbed, and the power they seem to have can only manifest itself against things of the same nature, it follows that the difference in concreteness between them and the intelligible universals could result equally from the greater concreteness of the latter. The mutual transformations and destructions of material things, which are so well adapted to impress the senses and

---

1. *Enneads*, III, 6, 6.

the imagination, can therefore prove the opposite of what they seem to prove for common sense.

The common sense delusion is almost inevitable because the imagination is far more closely attached to the material level than reason is, and common sense typically tries to confine thought to what can be imagined. The operation of reason, however, is exempt from all dependence on sense and images, whence its ability to discover and define the real nature of material things.

SPIRITUALITY AND POWER

The choice of spiritual values can thus be seen as a choice of the greater concreteness and greater reality of the intelligible and unchanging instead of the material and the mutable. The ability to exercise some degree of choice in this connection would therefore amount to having a choice between greater and lesser realities, and the result of this choice will be either to increase the power of the will by joining its activity to the greater reality, or to weaken it by joining it to the lesser reality. The nature of the whole person becomes assimilated to that of the realities which most engage his will and understanding, for good or ill, depending on their degrees of reality.

From the standpoint of the soul, this choice is between realities which are similar by nature to the soul, on the one hand, or realities which are alien and inferior to it, on the other. The latter option is to attempt the impossibility of overcoming the difference between the self and the material world, that is between the soul and the things from which it forms its representation of the world.

Conversely, the choice of the higher values is in effect a withdrawal of activity from a self-defeating or even self-destructive direction of the will, and a transference of it to a state from whence its power can extend indefinitely in both manifest and unseen ways. Such a choice satisfies a need for self-development which is not achieved at the expense of any other beings, so that it can take away the desire for the cruder forms of dominance. It is ignorance of this which leads to the pursuit of power in its usual worldly forms. When, as usual, it is sincerely denied that the spiritual life involves power, this is really because (a) the word is being taken in the materialistic sense just referred to, and (b) because power is not likely to be achieved in this realm if it is one's *direct* object of pursuit. Such misunderstandings result from the mindset of cultures which are strongly affected by the vulgar pursuit of the grosser forms of power for their own sake.

The conclusion that a spiritually-grounded power depends on a kind of identification with eternal nonmaterial realities agrees with what has been said before about the material world and the soul's private representation of it. Not only is the world of sense known to us only through representations, but also the objects which cause them are, *qua* material, both of a lower degree of reality and inaccessible to us in their inner substance, precisely because for us they can only be represented. Where this is ignored, the real will be sought where it is least knowable, at the price of one's capacity for real knowledge.

Now that it is possible to see why common sense is deceived in believing the material world to be the measure of the real, it can be seen how this mistake is reinforced and propagated by the anti-dualist philosophies which deny the soul as an independent agent in relation to matter. If we are already deceived on this issue, anti-dualist thinking will leave no rational grounds for trying to find the true option. Conversely, dualism is no danger to the unity of the person when the soul is understood as its Form, and the body as the unique instantiation of that Form.

What has been said concerning the greater relative concreteness of the soul and its ideas can also be justified with reference to its relations to the Forms which are instantiated in the material world. Matter, it is said, receives the Forms, and by means of the powers thus lent to them, it acts upon the senses. This is commonly believed to be the only way in which we gain knowledge, because we ignore the prior existence of the essences of all knowledge in the soul. Such a way of thinking would inevitably make the soul subordinate in rank even to material objects, since they at least receive the Forms at first-hand.

Such a possibility, Proclus has explained, is not consistent with the fact that we can solve mathematical problems concerning such idealities as circles and triangles with a precision and a universality which are by no means present in any sensible circles or triangles. Likewise, the purity and stability of ideas such as equality, proportion, and number, cannot be owing to sensory knowledge, in which all is mixed, imprecise, and subject to constant change:

> We must therefore posit the soul as the genetrix of mathematical Forms and ideas. And if we say that the soul produces them by having their patterns in her own essence and that these offspring are the projections of Forms previously existing in her, we shall be in agreement with Plato.[2]

We shall also be in agreement with the status which has been argued for soul and ideas in relation to material reality, and which give grounds for values which are the negation of materialistic thought. The inversion of the usual scale of reality which this implies is at the heart of the difficulty which is found in Platonism, as compared with naturalistic philosophies, but its validity has been shown to be not too hard for reason to test. Traditionally, minds which could not cope with this departure from common sense adopted the philosophy of Aristotle. This is a spiritually negative choice, not least because the duality between the truly concrete spiritual realities and the deceptively concrete material ones is a necessary basis for the operation of free will, as will appear in what follows.

2. Proclus, *Commentary on the First Book of Euclid*, Prologue 1,13.

9

THE FREEDOM
OF THE WILL

CONFUSIONS ABOUT FREE WILL

Free will and its opposite, determinism, form a duality in human consciousness which parallels that of Providence and Fate in the world. It may be asked how, if either of these is a reality, can the other exist. The answer to this results from the range of complexity comprised in the human microcosm, extending from the natural order to that of divinity, which has been examined in the last two chapters.

There are two reasons why free will is more riddled with confusion than most subjects, one of which is precisely the fact that it mingles in all proportions with its opposite, physical determination, so that free will to any high degree is hardly ever achieved all at once, but has to grow by a long process of development. Confusion is thus increased by free-willists who argue as though a full-blown free will was the property of all, and by determinists who deny its existence outright, as though they had no need of it themselves. Both sides can point to case histories to illustrate their arguments, but they are equally missing the real issue, that of our being originally unfree, but with a nascent free will which can develop to its full potential under the right conditions.

Another reason for the problems with this idea lies in a common sense idea of free will which would define it simply as an ability to do one thing as easily as another. This is one of the least demonstrable ideas, since it could only be directly tested if one could do and not do the same thing at the same time. It is true that our feelings constantly tell us that we could do one thing as easily as another, such as walking down the left side of a street or the right, but the idea seems to have no scope beyond feeling. However, this does not mean that free will is an incoherent conception, because it can be defined in less confusing ways. There is a freedom of will which comes from its being an originating cause in itself and being free from obstruction.

On this basis, it could be free in a meaningful way, that is, free from determination by alien causes, at least in certain instances. Such a will would be a true causal agent, but clearly this agency would not necessarily include an ability to do one thing as easily as another. This would not increase the freedom, because there is no difficulty in the idea of being able to do different things equally easily *without* freedom, under the action of outside forces. In that case, the action would not be specifically our own, so that so-called freedom of indifference need not mean freedom at all. Every real act of free will must be solely self-caused, and this idea is more accessible to proof, subject to the duality of soul and body.

FREE WILL AND RELEASE FROM FATE

The relevance of proofs of free will can be better understood when its spiritual context is appreciated. Even if it were certain that man had a power of volition which proceeded from himself alone, that would not prevent the existence of innumerable external causes which could influence the will at the same time. This point connects with the idea that free will is usually very incomplete and that its full realization is a long process. This process would consist in a progressive elimination, or at least subordination, of the alien causes which commonly manipulate the will, and a corresponding ascendancy of what is owing to the will alone. Such a process can be envisaged in alchemical terms as a removal of the 'dross' which allows the 'gold' concealed in it to appear in pure form.

These considerations apply to what philosophers have said about free will from the earliest times, where they speak of a double nature in the soul, which gives it an internal focus of choice:

the soul that descends to us from the worlds follows the periods of the worlds; but that which is intelligibly present from the intelligible transcends the genesiurgic motion, and through this a liberation from fate, and the ascent to the intelligible Gods, are effected.[1]

Here, 'that which is intelligibly present from the intelligible' was the subject of the last two chapters, which show that there is no self-contradiction in speaking of both 'fate' and 'liberation from fate.' They are both realities because the real is not confined to a single level or a single dimension.

Given that the true answer is in terms of a *conditional* free will, the next passage after the above further clarifies the issue, and the point is not affected by its reference to the Gods rather than to God. The relation between religion and philosophy expressed here is of universal significance:

Hence that of which you are dubious is not true, 'that all things are bound with indissoluble bonds of Necessity,' which we call Fate. For the soul has a proper principle of circumduction to the intelligible, and of a separation from generated natures; and also of a contact with real being, and that which is divine. 'Nor must we ascribe fate to the Gods, whom we worship in temples and statues, as the dissolvers of fate.' For the Gods, indeed, dissolve fate; but the last natures which proceed from them, and are complicated with the generation of the world and with the body, give completion to fate. Hence we very properly worship the Gods with all possible sanctity, and the observance of all religious rites, in order that they may liberate us from the evils impending from fate, as they alone rule over necessity through intellectual persuasion. But neither are all things comprehended in the nature of fate, but there is another principle of the soul, which is superior to all nature and generation, and through which we are capable of being united to the Gods, of transcending the mundane order, and of participating eternal life, and the energy of

---

1. Iamblichus, *On the Mysteries*, VIII, chap. VI, Thomas Taylor, tr.

the super-celestial Gods. Through this principle, therefore, we are able to liberate ourselves from fate.[2]

The reference here is to the 'divine spark' of the soul, or the *synteresis*, which is the counterpoise to the soul's involvement in the material world. Because of its presence, the human state contains something of all levels of being, including even the divine.

ARGUMENTS FOR FREE WILL

In the normal natural state, freely-willed and unfree actions mingle in all proportions, because external causes can condition one's will in proportion to one's lack of self-awareness. This very failure of free will points to an argument against determinism, because the fact that natural causes can account for many acts of will can never exclude the action of yet more such causes at the same time, though at present they may be unknown. In any case, with the advance of science, the number of known natural causes acting on human behavior has grown steadily, so that it may appear that one day everything will be explained in terms of external causes. However, this increase in known causes is in principle infinitely extensible, as nothing ever indicates an upper limit to the number of contributory causes; and yet for determinism to be true, it must be possible to specify an exact number of causes to account for any given action. Free will can never be excluded as long as there is room for the addition of one more cause, therefore. Free will would involve the addition of an 'uncaused cause' owing to our will alone, and there is nothing known about the external causes which could exclude this. (The opposite of the uncaused cause has already been encountered in connection with representations, which are caused, but without having any causal action of their own).

Consequently, given at least an element of free will, such a will can act in ways which will result in either more or less scope for its own action. There is a criterion by which this 'more' or 'less' may be judged. Since the hypothetically free (uncaused) will is in any case

2. Ibid., chap. VII.

just one of a number of forces influencing one's behavior, the will is situated at the center of many outside forces which are not all compatible with one another. To decide for any one of them will be to decide against the others.

It is not surprising that the number of potential causes should so exceed the number of possible effects, as can be seen in the example of the oak tree which sheds countless acorns, few of which become other oak trees. Besides, there are important differences among the causal forces which may or may not be allowed to act. For example, some of them may be compatible with the plan of one's life as a whole, while others may not. Similarly, some may be in accordance with values and principles, while others may be purely and simply random natural forces which manifest only the functioning of the macrocosm.

Because of the presence of its immanent principle or 'divine spark', the soul can thus align itself with forces and influences which share its true nature, or it can align itself with forces which are alien to it and which tend to make it more and more a part of a physical system in which individuality would ultimately be lost. In the former case, the will becomes increasingly free because it tends to a self-constituted or autarchic state, while in the latter it grows less free through being reduced to a minority position among a crowd of competing natural forces.

For this reason, the use of a mediocre degree of free will can lead either to successively higher degrees of free will or reduce it to a minimal functioning which may be ignored by scientific observation. The less free the will is, the more it functions simply in reaction to outside forces with standard responses to standard stimuli and situations. This may suffice for one to individuate as a 'type,' but not as full person. Such minimal use of free will is made more prevalent by the fact that socially integrative behavior does not arouse any opposition, so that the meaning of the individual life can be sidelined almost unawares.

The more the will is free, the more it is capable of consistent and self-originated activity, and the less it has merely to react. Three elements can be discerned in freely-willed activity, namely, the physical strength necessary for it, a practical knowledge of what the action involves, and finally a relation of the action to values and long-term purpose, not to accidental needs and whims. These conditions are clearly separable, since actions can be performed in blind ignorance or delusion, or one could combine the first two of these conditions in a well-planned crime, for example. But real freely-willed action requires all three conditions.

The freedom of the will not only does not conflict with universal natural causality, it is itself a cause. If this were not the case, the will would be nothing in relation to natural causes, and there could be no reason to speak of its freedom. Actions and decisions caused by the will usually appear with hindsight to be the outcome of previous external causes, among which the will has made a selection and excluded all but one or two in any given case. This is possible because of the excess of potential causes over possible effects referred to above. The will is in effect a cause which acts on other causes, having a superior position among them. When there are external causes both to lie and to tell the truth, for example, the causality of the will decides which is to produce its effect.

It has already been pointed out that the idea of freedom of indifference, or the ability to do one thing as easily as another, is an obscure idea which comes from feeling rather than reason. In addition to this, there is also confusion in the common sense idea that the true field of free will lies among concrete objects, encounters, and practical choices. Undeniably, free will has a role in such things, but it is far from being an optimal one. This is because practical life by definition brings us to situations, events and demands which we have no power either to create or to avoid, and upon such things we are dependent for the exercise of our free will in the world.

Because of this dependence, there can be no absolute free will in the world of practicalities. The doctor depends on the occurrence of sicknesses so as to use his skill, while the soldier and the politician depend similarly on the troubles they are trained to deal with. This constant dependence indicates that it is only a semi-free will which engages in practical affairs. The latter are typically cases where one is confronted with alternatives A and B, which one is obliged to understand and choose between. Full free will, therefore, belongs to a state in which choice is not necessary, but can itself be chosen. No options

A and B are dictated to it, but it can choose the situation containing A and B, along with the choice to be made between them. From such an unconditioned state, choices can have an absolute merit or guilt, which they cannot have in practical life.

This does not mean that as much freedom is involved in doing wrong as in doing right. The Fall took place, it is said, because Adam and Eve had the free will to disobey. However, in the light of what has been said as to the three conditions for complete free will and the uses by which it is reduced or lost, it can be seen that their disobedience resulted from the incompleteness of their free will, and not from their free will as such.

If full free will involves causal power, circumstantial knowledge, and a relation to ultimate value, it follows that morally wrong actions can have at most only the first two of these conditions, and even the second rather imperfectly. A classic example of this is Oedipus' murder of his father and marriage to his mother. He had the power to effect these things, but his understanding of the situation in which they were done was practically non-existent. The third condition, that of values, was no more involved, because he was moved only by a supposed practical expediency.

Thus although some elements of free will were present in his actions, they were freely-willed in only the most minimal sense because of his ignorance. The same observation applies to all morally bad or defective actions. Their necessarily lower degree of freedom argues a lower degree of responsibility and guilt, or would do so if there was no such thing as culpable ignorance. Some such previous failure of free will is normally a necessary condition for worse things.

The idea that the free will which is abused in wrongdoing can only be a deficient one is also a part of tradition. Saint Augustine, at the end of the last book of *The City of God*, recognizes this, and concludes that the saved in Heaven would no longer be able to sin, owing to their will having become perfectly free, a freedom which Adam and Eve never had in its fullness.[3]

---

3. St Augustine, *The City of God*, bk. XXII, chap. XXX.

FREE WILL AND KNOWLEDGE OF TRUTH

One may deduce free will from a position where it is first of all ruled out: suppose all experiences of free will were simply disguised forms of causal determination. In this case, all that we think and say would occur as a result of physical causality, and this would include the statement that determinism is true. That would mean that we cannot argue for determinism as a consequence of its truth, but only as a consequence of physical forces. It may be supposed that physical forces could cause us to speak the truth in some instances, but if that happened to be the case, how would the fact become known to us? Suppose some chemical reaction in the brain makes people say that two twos make four, and an observer wishes to see whether or not they have been induced to utter a truth. Either his brain will function like theirs, in which case his judgement of this statement will likewise be solely the effect of a chemical reaction, and therefore unable to add any further weight to it; or he will be able to make a judgement which is caused by the truth of its content and not by physical forces. In this case, there would be true confirmation that the statement was true, but if this can be granted to the observer, there will be no reason for denying it to everyone else, which contradicts the original premise that only natural causes make us say that some things are true, whence the supposed physical origin of thought must be an irrelevance.

The fact remains, then, that were determinism true, we should be declaring it to be true for *reasons other than the truth of this statement*, in which case we should not be logically bound to believe or heed it. No matter how subtle the causality involved, the resulting statement would be as little relevant as if it were induced by drugs, hypnosis, or bribery. Reason has a necessity peculiar to itself, of course, but the point at issue is that this necessity is one of a fundamentally different kind from the physical.

Now, the very existence of physical laws and forces is known only as a result of reasoning, which by definition must be determined only by truth. So if reason were in reality just a special case of physical causality, we should be led to the position that physical forces must have the power to induce a belief in their reality outside any independent power of judgement. But this believing, as much as knowing, would also be only a biochemical by-product, leaving it with no rational basis, and the nemesis of determinism is complete. In reality, it is only possible to know physical causality for what it is because the mind is determined by something quite different from physical causality.

But how does freedom enter into this? Are there not thus two orders of necessity and nothing else? Freedom arises from the fact that human nature contains both of these dimensions, and that there is no compulsion to operate under either to the exclusion of the other. Besides this, there is the Kantian consideration that when man is governed by the necessity of reason, rather than that of nature, he is not under any alien domination, but is walking by his own light. The law of reason is the law which logically precedes the laws of natural forces, so that conformity to reason joins the will to the power which governs those forces, and the ability to rule over the natural order in this inward manner is experienced as freedom. Here again, there is a spiritual conception of power, one which connects with what has been deduced about it already. Freedom and true power express the same thing from different points of view.

This account of free will depends on a dualistic conception which divides the rational nature from the physical conditions of life. The idea that there is such an 'upper storey' to our being may look dubious to modern minds, but the basis for this idea has been outlined where the soul was shown to be the container of its representation of its world. There is thus no *physical* reality external to the soul. While its activity is modified by its relation to the senses on the ego level, its position as container of the physical world as we know it means that the soul itself is relative only to God and to other spiritual beings. This is why it has a level of volition which is autonomous in relation to the material world, in which it is free to obey only its own law, however much it may be determined by other things on the ego level.

The present subject is pivotal in relation to the work of intellect, since a free will is necessary if mental enlightenment is to have more than a momentary influence on the personality as a whole. Given an objective duality between rational and physical necessity, and man's involvement in both, the idea of liberation from fate refers to a real possibility. This mystically effectual aspect of human intelligence is what most distinguishes it from so-called artificial intelligence. In machines which are designed to imitate the effects of intelligence, there is no question of a tension between two modes of being, because artificial intelligence has by definition no will of its own - only that of its users.

What has been said about free will has not connected it with divine grace, but this does not affect what has been argued as to its essential nature. The question of grace arises from the fact that human free will has to grow from very limited beginnings, and hold its place in a world whose powers of change can outrun the capacities of the individual alone. The will in practice needs a spiritual counterpoise to the natural forces which oppose its self-realization.

If the above conception of free will is applied by analogy to God, it can be seen why God's free will must also be one of independent and unopposed causality, and not a freedom of indifference, as too often supposed. Otherwise, God would be subject to the human limitation of acting without adequate reasons. Besides, no pairs of alternatives could be equal in the light of omniscience, however equal they may appear to be to limited human faculties. Freedom is a power to engage with the truly real.

10

THE LAW OF
ACTION AND REACTION

SOURCES IN SCRIPTURE

There is no shortage of Biblical affirmations of this law:

God is not mocked, for whatever a man sows that he will also reap.[1]

Draw near to God and he will draw near to you.[2]

Judge not that ye be not judged. For with what judgement ye judge, ye shall be judged: and with what measure ye mete it shall be measured to you again.[3]

All they that take the sword shall perish by the sword.[4]

Whosoever shall deny me before men, him will I also deny before my Father which is in heaven.[5]

Cast thy bread upon the waters, for thou shalt find it after many days.[6]

Do no evil and evil will never befall you. Stay away from wrong and it will turn away from you.[7]

Whoso sheddeth man's blood, by man shall his blood be shed.[8]

1. Gal. 6:7.
2. James 4:8.
3. Matt. 7:1.
4. Matt. 26:52 and Rev. 13:10.
5. Matt. 10:32–33.
6. Eccl. 11:1.
7. Sirach 7:1–2.
8. Gen. 9:6.

These are scriptural examples of a universal law, which is found to apply on almost every level from the most subtle down to the most purely mechanical. But despite its universality, it is only in the mechanical realm that it receives its full measure of recognition, where it is enshrined in Newton's Third Law of Motion, to *every action there is an equal and opposite reaction*. This is because mechanical instances of this law are open to simple observation and experiment, where it is not hard to see that objects are stable because the forces holding them up are equal to their weights.

Conversely, in the realm of conscious events, observation is made harder by the closeness of their activity to our own minds. The Law of Action and Reaction, which I will simply refer to as the Law for brevity, would not apply so strictly to the material realm were it not part of an archetypal reality which is the formal cause of natural forces. But while there is an aesthetic sense that it is somehow appropriate, as the expression 'poetic justice' shows, there seem to be few means of making it any more intelligible. What makes it necessarily a law, as much for Providence as for physical forces? The answer lies in the law of cause and effect, of which it is a special instance. Despite philosophical criticism, the law of cause and effect remains indispensable for our understanding of our own experiences, so that it may well be an integral part of the human mind, as Kant maintains.

THE CAUSAL PRINCIPLE AND CONTINUITY

While it is inseparable from causality, the Law further implies a certain order and proportion in the ways in which effects proceed from causes. It also implies that on the physical plane, no one being can be exclusively either a cause or an effect, but must be both of them at different times or in different relations. The Law requires above all that there be an equilibrium between these relatively active and passive states. This equilibrium entails a relation of similitude or analogy between the actions of a given agent and the reactions which follow them. What one person is as an agent should in theory determine what other persons will be as agents in relation to him, though this in practice is confused by the variability of the timescale.

Different persons act with very different degrees of free will, and this also rules out any mechanically obvious pattern of action and reaction, since it means that physically similar actions can differ internally at the same time; the actions of conscious agents owe so much of their true nature to the beliefs and intentions with which they are performed. Another difference between spiritual and physical energies is that in the former, action and reaction are seldom single movements but are usually more or less complex accumulations of energy with a given tendency. The psychical energy needed to induce a verifiable reaction would thus result not from one but from an accumulation of actions of a given type. How many such actions may be required cannot be specified because they have too many variables in the qualities of their intentions and the strength of volition applied to them.

Nevertheless, every accumulation of energy with a given quality or tendency somehow draws to itself others of a like nature. This fact has been observed from ancient times, before philosophy as we know it, as where Homer says 'As ever, God is bringing like and like together.' Since it is ordained by God, this association of like beings with like comes from something more than their conscious intentions; their natural inclinations alone tend to something they do not know about. The problem is how to pursue the analysis of this idea beyond the truism that birds of a feather flock together.

Involved is something with an almost mathematical necessity arising from the general relation of cause and effect, a key to which is found in a law which applies to the order in which effects proceed from their causes, that the productive agency causes first of all things most like itself, and subsequently things decreasingly like it.

If the cause were to produce an effect so unlike itself that others more like it could have been placed in order before that effect, there would be an arbitrary breach in the scale of being, and the very connection between cause and effect would be in doubt. A simple example of this is the heat from a fire which is most like that of the fire itself at close proximity but which declines into lesser degrees of warmth with distance. A similar pattern appears in the functioning of nearly all artefacts, which serve their intended purpose when new, but gradually wear out.

This is to consider causality operating in one direction only, however, that is to say, solely *from* the cause and not back to it. But where the causal agent is a finite being, this could not take place permanently without his having the power unilaterally and arbitrarily to alter the world according to his own will and his own nature. In this case, finite causal agents would have a power like that of God, which would be self-contradictory. In reality, the finite power of created agents, together with the unity of the world-order, implies that every action must ultimately be matched or complemented by its like. Only in this way is the unity of the world conserved against the confusion that would result from many beings having a unilateral power. This 'reverting' activity which finite agents attract to themselves for good or ill may be supportive or destructive, depending on the case. Action which harmonizes with that of God as First Cause will bring about reactions of one kind, and action in conflict with it, another. In this way, community results from interior dispositions.

This counteracts the common sense belief that people have similar outlooks and aptitudes because they inhabit the same locality where they must adapt to one another. On a deeper level, those who share these external conditions are drawn into them and kept there by an inner tendency that may not be clearly recognized. Such is the 'silent road'[9] by which, according to Platonists, all beings gravitate to the outward states which correspond to those of their souls.

WHAT CONTROLS THE WORLD?

We need to bear in mind the two principles involved here, that of qualitative continuity among all things, and the general circulatory pattern of causal energies. All qualities which are common to two or more beings are so many doorways through which they can interact and have power in relation to one another. Conversely, a lack of common qualities and tendencies is a more substantial barrier between them than stone walls, no matter how odd this may seem to

9. *Enneads* IV, 4, 45.

materialistic thinking, for which human beings are seen as so many interchangeable units.

When we consider situations that chance may bring upon us, the tendency is to think as though chance were all-powerful, but even if this idea gets some apparent support from individuals who combine inconsistent and undeveloped tendencies in themselves, this appearance is deceptive. Any apparent randomness in the events that life is subject to is in fact preselected by a kind of randomness in the tendencies and purposes of those involved, whether this condition is voluntary or not. The outward life is a fruition of the inward self; here cause and effect reign undisturbed, whether the related states are of order or disorder.

As qualitative likeness brings beings into relation in the outside world, and as the strongest form of likeness is a similar mode of purpose and action, the encounter of likes and the non-encounter of unlikes are the more assured the more these individual tendencies are developed and confirmed. When this is appreciated, the verse in the *Tao Te Ching* which may appear only to assert that a peaceful person will have a peaceful kind of life, or something almost as trite, will be seen to be a clear statement of the Law, and to show that all interaction is made possible by a correspondence of natures:

> *As I have heard, the man who knows*
> *On land how best to be at peace*
> *Will never meet a tiger or a buffalo:*
> *In battle, weapons do not touch his skin;*
> *There is no place for the tiger's claws to grip;*
> *Or with his horn, the buffalo can jab;*
> *Or where the soldier can insert his sword.*
> *Why so? In him there is no place of death.*[10]

The 'place of death' in the person is the counterpart of a lethal tendency against the outside world. Encounters with hostile beings are in reality a cause for self reproach, because they are external realizations of inward evils. By keeping increasingly free from certain states of mind for long enough, one may exhaust the negative reactions

10. Lao Tzu, *Tao Te Ching*, chap. 50, R. B. Blakney, tr.

from the world which would need to connect with such corresponding inner states in order to be manifest. In this way, the 'cosmic debts' incurred by the use of negative energies can be dissipated.

The practical consequences of the Law, as manifest in this manner, are of special importance, since they throw light on the true and essential power of the individual which is never recognized by common sense. They involve a way of transcending the apparent helplessness of the isolated person in a way which reconciles his good with that of his world. By virtue of the Law, actions and orientations are never merely private, despite appearances. Consequently, a manner of being which deepens the relation to God and universal values, and so identifies with a more concrete reality, thus interacts with the ambient world simply by being part of it. This is to be the instrument of an action of presence which necessarily attracts proportionate positive action from the world, and so liberates potentialities within it which increase its order and stability.

This is why the security of any society depends on the presence in it of minorities and individuals who are spiritually alien to it, who have a mission which goes far beyond the basic practicalities which rest on everyone. In their absence, disastrous events and changes can spread like the plague through populations whose collective will has become merged with natural forces. The impersonal aspect of the effectiveness of prayer can also be understood by the same principle, since it too is among other things a form of directed energy in a system where energy is conserved. In such a system, the presence or absence of such a force must make an absolute and permanent difference to one's role in relation to the world as much as to God.

The fact that the Law operates with precision does not mean that it will always do so visibly in the same way. Even among individuals who live by the same values, their different origins and inheritances will alter its pattern, and in any case there is the great variability in the times involved, according as the circuit of causes is long or short. It is mainly because of the wide variations among these time intervals that the succession of action and reaction passes unnoticed. A major factor here is the degree to which true values inform one's life, and the way in which this affects its relation to God as Highest Cause. The return of reactions rapidly enough for them to be recognized as such is a sign of closeness to the truth, and conversely, the long or indefinite delay of them is a sign that one has strayed too far from the truth to be able to atone for wrongs in this life.

CAUSALITY INCLUDES FREE WILL.

The variability in the times of reactions is essentially a result of free will, which operates outside hard causality. The will's motives cause the corresponding actions without being enough to make those actions physically necessary, and just because the Law is rigorous, reactions also have the same causal freedom as the actions. Where they befall the deluded, they are taken to be meaningless accidents which are made grounds for complaints against the Providence which has been ignored. If this were not the case, and the periods of the cyclic returns were standard quantities, the avoidance of moral wrong would be physically determined, and would have no more moral meaning than the avoidance of any other physical danger.

One class of apparent exceptions to the Law is that of children, who inevitably are subject to many things that cannot be the result of their own previous actions. But the difficulty is only apparent, firstly because children are not really separate from their parents except in a physical sense, and do not become spiritually separate until they have used free will in the course of growing up. This means that children automatically share in the moral merits and demerits of their parents, and indirectly in those of the society they belong to. In this case, they are sure to encounter reactions which are owing to their parents and families, and they themselves are destined to pass on goods and evils in the same way. In this connection, there is a Confucian text which states that the penalties for sin incurred by parents are passed on to their children if they are not settled in this life:

In the case of crimes, the Spirits presiding over the life, according to their lightness or gravity, take away the culprit's periods of twelve years or of one hundred days. If at death there remains guilt unpunished, judgement extends to his posterity.[11]

This teaching is said by the commentator to be very ancient in the history of the ethical teaching of China. *The Tractate of Actions and Their Retributions*, quoted above, is as a whole a testimony to the importance of the Law in ancient China. As such, it is a significant parallel to the same teaching in our own tradition, since it has a dominant place in the Old Testament. The teaching that penalties for sin are inheritable is also manifest in the Biblical teaching that:

> I the Lord your God am a jealous God, visiting the iniquity of the fathers upon the children to the third and fourth generation of those who hate me, but showing mercy on thousands of those who love me.[12]

This text is well known or notorious, but the attention paid to its punitive aspect obscures the more neutral meaning, that having children can be a way of off-loading one's cosmic debts. Those who dislike this doctrine usually ignore its equal implication that rewards earned by the virtues of ancestors must also be inheritable. The act of inheriting life at all must mean inheriting both goods and evils from the ancestors, and to expect to receive only the good is a result of sentimentality. Where the earliest part of life is concerned, moreover, one cannot rule out the possibility in some cases of a reversal between action and reaction, that is to say, that some actions of adult life could be rewarded or punished pre-emptively.

But if the Law does not make it necessary that reactions should always take the same form as the actions they result from, how can it be absolute? The answer to this involves some of its most important implications. Action and reaction are usually, but not necessarily, on the same level, as where a good deed (or an offence) is repaid with another one like it. In other cases the reaction can be just as real but without any visible form. The Gospels speak exactly in accordance with the Law in this connection where one is warned against giving hospitality only to those who will return it directly, and where one is advised to give it rather to those who are not able to return it. This

11. *The Tractate of Actions and Their Reactions, The Texts of Taoism*, pt. ii, James Legge, tr.

12. Exod. 20:5.

teaching also depends on the validity of the Law, but with the development that the prevention of a reaction on the plane of the original action can only result in its emergence on another one, in this instance, outside the temporal condition of the action. By this means, energy of a given quality and tendency is not lost but transformed beyond impermanence.

In other cases, where it is a question of malign actions suffered, the refusal to avenge it means that the reactive energy blocked in this way will realize a corresponding good, and one which is again outside the realm of time and matter where the original action arose. Thus, what is known as the renunciation of worldly rewards for virtue is, more deeply understood, a further application of the principle that energy cannot be created or destroyed, so that the fruits of action can be realized on an eternal level by their prevention on the temporal. If this is not understood, the requirement for sacrificial choices will be seen to be tyrannical and irrational, whereas it is concerned only with the maximum fruition and preservation of good. Instead of localized and ephemeral effects, the Law can enable spiritually qualified actions and states to send their reverberations throughout the human race and beyond time.

A steady accumulation of power in relation to the environment results at the same time, owing to the progressive exhaustion of the hostile reactions which were occasioned by one's own negative potentialities and the ones which one had inherited. Such power can be the basis for the development of power in the more conventional sense of the word, though never the opposite way around. Conversely, it may be left in its essential state, doing its work unseen, and therefore so much the more securely.

This is the reality which makes all the usual conceptions of success and failure, effectiveness and ineffectiveness irrelevant, since these things all lie on the surface of things, where actions and reactions are obviously of the same kind. The unspiritual world-view is in this way a kind of 'flatland'. It is besides ultimately futile unless it can be connected effectively with a reality of a superior order to its own, and that is what a conscious use of the Law can bring about.

There is an apparent conflict between the operation of the Law and belief in a personal relation to God, who is also personal. If this should appear to have a depersonalizing effect on our idea of God, it should be remembered that almost any action of a human being can be shown to take place according to the laws of physiology, psychology, logic, and morality, without ceasing to be genuinely personal. Both perspectives are real and subsist together like the woof and warp of a fabric, and if this can be so for human beings, it can hardly be less so in relation to their Creator. The world is so made as to be governed on all levels by both free will and causality, and this includes relations between the human and the divine. God, though not bound to act through intermediaries, in practice nearly always does so. The law is one of the most important metaphysical laws, as it is a unifying principle in relation to the physical, psychical, and spiritual realms, and so is the medium of positive self-transformation. Besides its being a theorem taught by numerous Biblical texts, it is part of a world-wide wisdom tradition, as already indicated in other traditional sources, such as the Confucian *Doctrine of the Steadfast Mean*, which bears witness to the universality of the Law in the form of the Golden Rule: 'What you do not like done to yourself do not do to others.' This clearly corresponds to the same teaching in the Gospels.

The same idea is also to be found in another Chinese traditional text where it is said that the fullness of knowledge leads to sincerity of thought, which rectifies the heart and cultivates the person. This regulates the life of families and the provinces they live in, which in turn makes the whole kingdom peaceful and happy.[13] This latter point of view does not apparently extend to the ideals of self-denial and self-sacrifice, but it is nevertheless capable of an extension which can comprehend them both within the same universal truth, as the next development of the Law will show.

---

13. 'The Great Learning', *Bible of the World*, p 420.

11

CHOICE OF
THE LESSER EVIL

The subject of this chapter proceeds from that of the previous one where I have already mentioned the possibility of apparently breaking the Law of Action and Reaction by non-retaliation, such that the reaction must take place on some other level. This normally involves the choice of suffering a wrong rather than being the cause of one, or 'turning the other cheek,' which is all too often regarded as an impractical and irresponsible form of otherworldliness resulting from an over-literal reading of scripture.

Such is the ignorance and confusion with which this subject is surrounded that it can be confused with self-destructive and morbid forms of behavior which are really poles apart from the deeper consciousness which determines non-retaliation. This idea is also subject to political embarrassments today, because it seems well adapted to the purpose of helping those at the top of the tree to stay where they are, and of ensuring that those at the bottom stay where they are. If it was a way of telling losers that their condition was really good for them, it would of course suit the worldly interests of more advantaged groups, and pacify their conscience. The mere suspicion that what is involved here could be just a cost-effective way of solving social injustices, and one which would justify *inaction*, that bogey of the modern mind, has been enough to banish it from the pulpit.

However, the principle of non-retaliation, or nonresistance to evil, can be seen in a very different light in view of what has been said about causality and free will. The teaching in the Sermon on the Mount to 'Resist not one who is evil,' can be understood as a vital part of the universal metaphysical tradition, and one which unites the theoretical with the practical. When it is so understood, it can be seen to have nothing to do with either worldly opportunism or self-betrayal.

All human actions are examples of causal agency, and the basis on which they produce their effects is the same as for any other kind of cause. This is what will have to be examined more closely to make clear the logic of non-retaliation. An essential starting-point lies in a property of causality which is expressed by Proclus as follows:

> Every productive cause is superior to that which it produces, [and] were it able to fashion another thing more perfect than itself, it would make itself perfect before its consequent.[1]

The latter statement merely expresses the paradox involved in a denial of the former statement. Whatever is in the cause must reside there in some more powerful way than it does in the effect. This is necessary for causality itself, as the alternative would mean the production of something from nothing. Cause and effect cannot be equal either, since this would give rise to an infinite series of beings, each one of which was equal to the last, each being as much a cause as it was an effect, and the last of which would have powers equal to those of the first. Needless to say, no such infinite multiplication is ever experienced, and neither could the world contain it.

The actual decline of power from cause to effect is illustrated by most kinds of effect as, for example, a fire must be very hot just in order to produce a moderate warmth at a given distance; a source of light must have a brightness many times that of its reflected light by which we see the things it illuminates; a thorough understanding of something is necessary in order to convey a moderate understanding of it to others.

Such examples agree with an intuitive sense that a certain loss is involved in all such processes, and the significance of this for the present purpose will appear when we take the human will as an

---

1. Proclus, *Elements of Theology*, prop. 7.

example of a cause, acting so as to cause either good or evil. The result of this is far less close to common sense, however, since it follows that if anyone suffers an injustice by the act of someone else's will, the mere fact that it is an effect means that the evil he finds in it must somehow be less than the corresponding evil in the will which has caused it, according to what has just been explained. No matter how great the evil which is suffered, then, it must always be still greater in the person who has caused it.

THE INSENTIENCE OF THE ACTIVE FACULTIES

At first sight, this seems open to the objection that, were it true, everyone would avoid harming others even more than they avoided harm to themselves. Nevertheless, this is a mistake arising from the role of feeling, which functions in quite different ways on either side of this issue. The causing of a wrong, as with the causing of any other effect, comes from the purely active faculties of mind and will, which are *per se* insentient, while the suffering of an action is first and foremost a matter for the mainly passive faculties, i.e., the senses, the emotions, and the imagination. This means that the reception of an evil is inevitably accompanied by a corresponding emotional reaction, while the infliction of it requires no such reaction, even though it bears the greater evil.

If, therefore, we judge subjectively, and do not look beyond feeling, we can easily suppose that the evil must be one-sidedly present in those who suffer it. Yet in reality, it not only exists in the agent to a greater degree, but it also infects the most essential part of his personality, the one by which the whole person can be made good or bad. Conversely, no possible degree of evil suffered by the outer personality could ever suffice to make the sufferer himself evil, provided only that his will is not moved to retaliate. There is in fact no necessary connection between suffering an injustice and becoming minded to imitate the action. One can always allow the wrong to rest where it was first experienced and give it no access to the more spiritual part of the self.

The causation of good or evil can proceed from the mind and will of one person to the sensibility of another, or from the mind and will to the sensibility of one and the same person, and in the case of evil, the greater of the two evils is relatively anesthetized, for the above reason. Besides the fundamental reasons given, moreover, the working of the Law ensures that the reaction of retaliation which is withheld must ultimately assume a form which is to the advantage of the one who withholds it, to an extent proportional to its original potential for evil.

This makes it as great a certainty as anything the so-called exact sciences can offer, and it requires no theological, moral, or utilitarian considerations to complete its case. Its scriptural authority exactly matches the metaphysical certainty which belongs to this central issue of human life and destiny. Plato gave a proof of it in the *Gorgias* dialogue, but it is too convoluted to be convincing, and depends too much on the finer shades of word-meanings. Since Plato, the attempt to establish it as a logical certainty has been all but abandoned, although the solution is not hard to grasp.

COSMIC REACTION AND JUDGEMENT

Non-retaliation is by no means confined to Christian tradition, as can be seen from a Sufic text quoted by Fabre d'Olivet in his book on the Golden Verses of Pythagoras:

> Learn of the sea-shell to love thine enemy, and to fill with pearls the hand thrust out to harm thee. Be not less generous than the hard rock; make resplendent with precious stones the arm which rends thy side.[2]

Once this principle has been understood theoretically, it must be understood in practice, where it can raise problems which can nevertheless be solved in terms of the Law. The most obvious misunderstanding is that non-resistance must mean making oneself liable to unlimited amounts of injury from all quarters, rather as when Socrates was told that his pursuit of philosophy meant only that anyone who wished could box his ears. However, this supposition is

---

2. Fabre d'Olivet, *The Golden Verses of Pythagoras*, chap. 11.

really only superficial because it ignores the consequence of the Law that what man suffers is primarily the more or less delayed effect of his own previous actions.

If, after having lived by unjust, fraudulent or violent means, a sudden conversion to non-retaliation left someone exposed to the same kind of offences until the 'debts' had been cleared, the blame does not lie with the Law. On the contrary, the same principle which entails penalties entails a freedom from them when the direction of the life has changed for the good for a sufficient length of time.

Even though it may not be humanly possible to live so that no retaliation from outside world is ever occasioned, and though some persons may even provoke it in their pursuit of a good which outweighs their own security, there is still a clear difference between such cases and those where it is wrong-doing which brings negative reactions on those responsible for it. In the latter case, the evil of the reaction befalls the individual regardless of his intentions at the time when the reaction catches up with him; whereas in the former case, it can be an event which has been knowingly undertaken for a self-transcending purpose. The example of martyrs shows this, and theirs is an example of individuals choosing to go beyond the usual norms. Such cases in no way invalidate the Law, since one can always provoke a reaction which would not have been caused by the state of one's life in itself. In such cases, the Law's equilibrium will transform the natural evil into a spiritual good because a natural evil which occurs without any corresponding cause for it in the person realizes an equivalent good, given the right intentions.

The principle of non-retaliation depends for its spiritual effectiveness on there being no exceptions to the Law, which can be denied only in appearance, and temporarily. Its transformative function has already been indicated, and yet the question of the meaning of self-sacrifice is not the only one which arises here because the supremacy of the Law is often felt to be opposed by Christ's answer to the question as to whether those killed by the Tower of Siloam were worse sinners than the rest of the population.[3] He said that they were not, but this is of no help to those who wish to deny the relevance of the

3. Luke 13:4–5.

Law, because in the very next verse, those present were told that they would perish likewise if they did not repent. Christ thus actually affirms the connection between sin and natural evil, only with the caution that when cosmic reactions are due, they do not necessarily happen all at once to everyone who deserves them, or in easily-recognized patterns.

This idea of divine judgement in the world, with rewards and punishments falling where deserved, is practically as old as religion itself. It has long been a favorite target for sceptics, with the result that in modern times it is usually ignored, but at the price of giving up something essential to religion. Far from being just a materialistic concern for worldly rewards, this belief springs from a much deeper issue, namely, *that the world-order is moral*, despite all contrary appearances. This has always been the cornerstone of religious belief, and it is as necessary for Christianity as for the earlier religions. In the ninth century BC, Hesiod wrote that in lands where righteousness prevailed, nature was benign, and crops were abundant, as though there were a sympathetic relation between mankind and nature. That this seemed equally natural to Christians is illustrated by a rationalist historian as follows:

St Ambrose confidently asserted that the death of Maximus was a consequence of the crime he had committed in compelling the Christians to rebuild a Jewish Synagogue they had destroyed. A volcanic eruption that broke out at the commencement of the iconoclastic persecution was adduced as a clear proof that Divine anger was aroused, according to one party, by the hostility of the emperor to the sacred images.[4]

This author is using these examples to pour scorn on the idea of particular providence because he knows how essential it is for religion. But while it is easy to smile at the extravagances and contradictions that result from incautious appeals to the Law, such examples only mean that it must be applied in an informed and critical manner. The reasons for resisting the sceptic include the metaphysical certainty of the Law of Action and Reaction, the authority

4. W. E. H. Lecky, *A History of European Morals*, vol. 1, chap. 3.

of the Bible, and the objective nature of ultimate values discussed in chapter 7, which includes the moral nature of the world-order.

As regards Biblical authority, it has to be acknowledged that the Law's application to the attribution of worldly disasters and personal misfortunes to offences against the Commandments occurs on practically every other page of the Old Testament and numerous times in the New. One can safely say that no other principle is witnessed to more often in scripture, from the expulsion of Adam and Eve from Eden to the seven last plagues of the Apocalypse. Therefore, to reject this way of understanding the world, and to resign everything to the play of natural forces, is to part ways with revelation and the sacred tradition based on it.

The typical result of this rejection is the idea of an irrefutable God, one whose presence cannot be seen in actual events, whether individual or collective, and it is not hard to see what a stifling effect this has on religious faith. When everything is believed to happen because of natural forces alone without relation to value, the experience of the validity of belief is cut off from the outside world, and made exclusively part of the individual's relation to him or herself. For some idealistic minds, this seems acceptable because it ought to purify religion of everything which could appeal to self-interest (waiving the question as to whether finding salvation is in one's best interests).

This, however, involves one of the deep contradictions of modern thought. If all consequences of beliefs and actions had to await the hereafter, the result would be an impassable divide between the temporal life and the eternal, which must be anathema to the anti-dualistic thought of today, besides which it is the function of revealed religion to bridge such divisions. A certain kind of Deistic religion could persist on this basis, but its popular relevance would be nil.

CONSEQUENCES FOR MODERN RELIGION

As the main stream of modern Christianity seems to be agreed in ignoring the idea of particular providence or Divine judgement, despite the inner logic of Theism and its metaphysical dimension, we need to understand what must follow from this. Such is the popular indifference to the doctrinal basis of practical values that few will be offended at the idea that the God who is worshipped on this basis can only be the clockmaker God of Deism, who winds up the universe, sets it going, and then plays no further part in it. And yet the attempt to continue Theistic religion on this basis is at best a confusion, and at worst fraudulent. Theistic religion does not logically combine with the idea of reality common to Stoics and Epicureans which is implicit in Deism, and neither can it do so practically in the long run.

Instead of there being any admission of an adoption of Deism, the prevailing teaching is rather that particular providence still exists, if only in the choices and decisions made by individuals in regard to their spiritual condition. While the events that befall people in the outside world may not be willed by God except inasmuch as the world itself is willed, may it not still be true that our moral choices can still come about as responses to particular acts of the Divine will? If this were the case, there would be as complete a split between the inner and outer worlds as any conceived by Descartes. Contemporary religious teachings could only incorporate such an idea at the price of coherence. Nevertheless, it means that the charge of Deism can be evaded, as long as the individual mind is a haven where providential action can be believed in without attracting sceptical criticism.

This position requires the assumption that God acts on a part of the self which does not involve the body as such, although a choice, once made, must pass into action in a way which necessarily involves the physical with the spiritual, such that they cannot truly be separated. In this case, there is no point in denying God's action on the outside world as well.

The idea of providential action on human minds alone is also bound up with the common sense belief that there is an absolute distinction between events which we will to happen and events which happen to us, or between options we choose and options which confront us. This distinction serves practical purposes, but will not stand up to study in depth. The things that happen to us are as much expressions of our will as those which we will consciously.

The events to which we are passive are neither more nor less than the longer-term results of our own choices, since external relations arise only in response to corresponding realities in the inward disposition. Here again, there is no basis for trying to make conscious choices independent of physical events, even though mind has the possibility of dominating this relationship.

A particular Providence, therefore, must manifest itself through specific acts on both our interior states and on external happenings, or on neither. A form of doctrine which denies all Dualism does not in any case have the option of a purely spiritual realm to which the Divine action could be confined. Such a position is irrational, and is most probably inspired by the fear that if the substantive or nine-tenths Deism of modern religious thought was seen for what it was, the heresy involved would become apparent even to the general public.

Biblical tradition is so steeped in the conception of moral and spiritual goods leading to natural or material goods, and moral and spiritual evils leading to natural evils, that those who reject it are limiting the content of their belief in God so much that they are scarcely believers at all. Their influence on present-day forms of religious belief is the kind of paradox which one would naturally associate with the Last Times. Such minds are a perennial social reality, of course, since those who professed a belief in the Gods but denied that they ever tried to influence anything in this world were well known to Plato, who refused to distinguish them from atheists.

A related aspect of this issue is the effectuality of prayer, because the difference between God's response to prayer and God's intervening justice in the world, exists from the human point of view but not from the Divine, since no more is involved in either case than a response to manifestations of the human will. The physical scale of the intervention is likewise only an issue from the human point of view, as it has no meaning for omnipotence. Particular Providence and the effect of prayer are inseparable, and the denial of either must mean the denial of both. This is why the modern attitude in this connection effectively does away with the difference between religion and philosophy while the outward functions of religion remain.

The idea that life's outward changes and chances mirror one's inward and spiritual state may be rejected because of the example of martyrs, but in this case one confuses evils which result from ignorant and foolish choices and those which result from choices moved by a higher wisdom. A world in which anything could happen to anyone would be one in which the natural order was inherently amoral, and the commandments of religion would not make any concrete difference. Far from meaning an openness to Providence, it would really mean no Providence at all. It would even mean a denial of the redemptive power of suffering, since that depends on the absoluteness of the Law; subject to it, evils undergone with no moral cause in the victim are necessarily 'actions' which cause a like degree of good by way of reaction, if taken with the right understanding. The Law is proved even by cases which seem to deny it.

The conclusion that every evil is greater for the agent of it than for the patient, with its consequence of returning good for evil, or non-retaliation at least, harmonizes with what was said in relation to apparent breaches of the Law. Because it admits no exceptions, and energy is not created or destroyed, the withholding of a negative reaction does not mean the annihilation of a will or purpose, but its transformation. Here, then, is a second fundamental reason for this ethical code.

Insofar as this transformation of energy also determines the kinds of reactions that can return upon the individual, this ethic includes a means of exerting a benign control over the outside world which also frees one from it. Testimony to an awareness as to how the Law and non-retaliation work together can be found in the *Philokalia*, where it can be seen that more was involved than a purely personal morality. States of mind create a metaphysical bond between those involved:

> The cause of every distressing event is the thoughts of each one of us. I could have said words and deeds as well; but since they do not occur before thought, I ascribe all to thoughts.... The taking of one's neighbor upon oneself from malice is involuntary. And it happens thus: a man who deprives (his neighbor) of something takes upon himself the trial of him whom he has

deprived, even though he does not wish it; similarly, the slanderer—the trials of the slandered, the defrauder—those of the defrauded, the oppressor those of the oppressed.... The Divine Scriptures testify to this, saying, 'He that digs a pit for his neighbor shall fall into it: and he that rolls a stone rolls it upon himself. (Prov. 16:27)[5]

The particular merit of this text is that it illustrates the idea that external events are really physical reactions to mental causes, while at the same time connecting this with the Law of Action and Reaction. If Providence could be said to have a mechanism for its process of transformation and regeneration, this must surely be it.

5. *Philokalia*, St Mark the Ascetic, §§ 59–60, Palmer and Kadlubovsky, eds.

12

PROVIDENCE AND FATE

TWO FORMS OF COSMIC ORDER

Providence and Fate are two universal conceptions by which the world-order is interpreted, but despite their familiarity they are often misunderstood as a result of their being used in isolation from one another. In reality there is a very close connection between them, without which neither can be fully understood, whence it would be a mistake to treat either in isolation, in much the same way as it would be a mistake to explain magnetism without reference to electricity or vice-versa.

It may be asked why an archaic-sounding word like 'Fate' should be used, associated as it is with ancient forms of religion and drama. One could use the word 'nature' instead, but this word includes too much, especially in view of there being no sharp boundary between the natural and the supernatural. The essential fact is that there is much about human life which is necessarily the same for all: a cycle of birth, growth, maturity, decline, and death, and everything attendant on these things. This groundwork of invariants, which is not much affected by individual qualities, is most aptly referred to as our 'fate.' The question is not whether this fate could be escaped at its own level, but whether we are wholly subject to it, or only partially, and whether it can be transformed from within. What has been said about the natural transcendence peculiar to consciousness suggests one kind of answer.

Given that there is no hard and fast division between the natural and the supernatural, a normal human life partakes of both to varying degrees, and this is why it is so hard to distinguish between the providential and the fatal in life, even though the distinction is a fundamental one. The differences between them are not hard to express in general outline, since Fate refers to a kind of order manifest as necessity, constraint, and a coercive causality, which includes purely random events. Under Fate, only the whole system has a purpose; individual beings subject to it are merely means to its ends. Conversely, Providence comprises a different kind of order, one which combines with freedom, albeit a freedom with laws peculiar to itself, by means of which individual beings can realize purposes which are their own, and not those of the cosmic system. The absence of this freedom under Fate means that its place is occupied by what could be called its shadow, the arbitrariness of chance events. For this reason, supposedly spiritual teachings for which the total system is the only real agent are only disguised expressions of Fate.

Where the providential freedom is effective, it is manifest in the ordering of things by a benign intelligence which leads souls to a good which seems to have been pre-ordained for them, or for which they seem to have been made. But if Fate and Providence are both realities, it is necessary to understand how they can subsist together without neutralizing one another. An indication that they are complementary and not antagonistic can be seen from the fact that we should not experience Fate as a constraining force unless there were something in us which did not belong to it, and that, conversely, the freedom ascribed to Providence would have little or no meaning unless the world contained an objective unfreedom as well. Unless their distinction is made intelligible, attempts to discuss either or both of them will amount only to using different terms for the same things. If everything is included under one or other of these two orders, the only result is to make it a mere synonym for 'the world' or 'the total system', explaining nothing.

PROVIDENCE AND ARCHETYPAL REALITY

The dichotomy involved in this is far from being a man-made problem. It arises logically from the basic conceptions of an order of subsistent values which make up the pre-existent pattern of the world as conceived by its Creator, on the one hand, and from the realm of physical interactions between the material instantiations of these eternal patterns on the other. This involves the usual Platonic distinction between the Forms and their instances which is often treated by Christian thought as the relation between the eternal ideas in the divine mind and the created world.

The material world is in a sense a duplicate of the spiritual world, as all its contents correspond, in however limited a way, to those of the latter. Both as a whole and in its parts it derives from the Forms, but the relationships between the entities in it often fail to be instances of the relations between their Forms, however. Their relations may be disordered by a physical causality which can work independently within certain limits. Not only do things fall short of their archetypal causes, but the identities of physical beings are also variable because there is more in their Forms than can be manifest by them at any given time, though these different possibilities are by no means of equal value in relation to them. Natural causality thus has scope for changing beings in ways which may or may not answer to their most essential possibilities. Natural causes operate with a necessity and a regularity which goes with the lack of consciousness and individual purpose which is proper to the material state as such. This unconscious and unfree level of being is sometimes known as *natura naturata*, in contrast to that of the Forms, which are *natura naturans*.

But since Providence includes *natura naturans*, it is also the agency by which the Forms of individuals become not merely instantiated, but instantiated to the fullest degree. For this reason, the Catholic idea of co-operating with Providence is linked to the idea of realizing one's individual Form or Exemplar:

> The divine action executes in time the ideas which the eternal wisdom has formed of all things. All things have in God their own ideas.... The divine action sees in the Word the idea in accordance with which you have to be formed; this idea is your exemplar.[1]

This expresses a kind of predestination inasmuch as an architect's plan predestines the building of a house, though this conception

---

1. J. P. de Caussade, *Self-Abandonment to Divine Providence*, bk. 1, chap. 2, 12.

gives no grounds or meaning for a negative predestination, because the idea of a plan for a building operation to fail would be a contradiction. As the above quotation indicates, the action of Providence is directed to individual intelligent beings qua individuals, for their own sake. This applies to intelligent beings because, as Aquinas expresses it:

> Things that are nearer the end fall more definitely under the order which is for the end, for by their mediation other things are also ordered to the end. . . . So the actions of intellectual substances more definitely fall under the order of Providence than the actions of other things.[2]

This indicates another distinction between the providential and the fatidic realms; what is subject to Fate is governed solely in regard to its function as a part of some wider category and not as an individual, rather in the way that bees are only cared for as a swarm, or cattle as a herd. As such, they are still subject to Providence, but only because Fate as a whole is subject to it. This point is made by Proclus as follows:

> Providence subsists prior to Fate, and all that is produced according to Fate is by a much greater priority produced by Providence, but the contrary is not true. [3]

The spiritual soul is capable of dependence on Providence directly, whereas the body depends on it primarily via Fate, which is said to preside over 'alter-motive and corporeal natures.' Providence governs both intellectual and corporeal natures, while Fate governs only the corporeal; the relation of these two precisely parallels that between intelligible realities and sensory ones.

Aquinas draws the same distinction:

> A rational creature exists under divine Providence as a being governed and provided for in himself, and not simply for the sake of his species, as is the case with other corruptible creatures.[4]

---

2. Aquinas, *SCG*, III, chap. 90, [5].
3. Proclus, *Providence and Fate*, §3.
4. *SCG*, III, chap. 113, [1].

It is part of the definition of the 'rational creature' that its possibilities correspond to the whole of reality, so that it is *per se* a whole analogous to the world itself. This, however, does not directly affect the status of the body, whose material constituents remain a part in relation to the biosphere in accordance with its determination by Fate. Creatures without the intelligence which typifies the spirit exist solely as parts, not only with their bodies but in their entirety, despite the fact that animals have individual characters which are just as unique in their own way as are those of human beings. If this should seem paradoxical, it should be realized that individuation, even unique individuation, does not suffice by itself for a true individuality. Grains of sand and snowflakes are all individuated without being in any meaningful sense individuals. Individuality requires a self-originated activity by which the individual is the source of his own actions.

To the extent that his actions partake of this principle of free will (and there are many different degrees to which they may do so), he effectually emerges from the conditioning forces of species and environment. This is something animals never do because they never truly act, but only react to sensory stimuli. Thus the ability to take action on the basis of things known outside any immediate relationship, along with rationality, makes the rational being effectively a 'little world' over against the natural order, such that he cannot be reducible to a mere part of anything in nature.

Another consequence of this is that the more fully one is subject to Providence, the more one shares in its power over Fate and can hold the balance between them. The most extreme and striking examples of this are to be seen in certain saints who were able to work miracles or convert many other persons. Their denials that such things were owing to any power of their own would also follow from this idea of the self with its participation in Providence. The opposite alternative to this spiritual governance of Fate is that of being ruled by it as a part of some general class of creatures, whence the soul's cosmic role is that of a mediator bridging the duality of body and intellect. In this way, it brings the Providential action directly into the material world:

For again, if intellect and deity are prior to soul, but passions and bodies are posterior to it; and if to these [the latter] it belongs to act from compulsion, but to intellect and deity, to act in a manner better than all necessity, and which alone is free, it is necessary that the soul betaking itself either to the former or to the latter, should either enter under the necessity of subordinate, or exert the liberty of more excellent natures; and that it should be subservient either to a supernal dominion, or to a dominion inferior to itself . . . it must either rule in conjunction with the powers that rule over it, or be alone subservient in conjunction with subservient natures.[5]

Every life is a combination of these two alternatives in one proportion or another, and they correspond to two ways of using the will, one of which is originative, while the other is merely transmissive. Here again is the apparent paradox that the authentic individual self results from an identification with a divine reality.

FATE, PROVIDENCE, AND SALVATION

What the soul needs to be saved from is a self-assimilation to Fate which tends to become increasingly exclusive of Providence. Subject to this condition, the will operates in a distinctive manner which follows the patterns of natural attractions and repulsions, in a way which stifles awareness of the self's potential power The more it is thus an instrument of natural forces, the less it can be a force in its own right, and as such it is actually unfree, regardless of what it may be in principle. For external observation, such a will can appear to be very active, but in the true sense of causing, initiating, or selecting activities, it is not active at all, in which case it is neither fully voluntary nor truly personal.

When the soul relates to externals in this way, it must relate in the same way to its own internal stimuli or passions, which are themselves rooted in changes that take place in the outside world, whether they be human or cosmic. In this connection, Aquinas admits the

5. Proclus, *Providence and Fate*, §18.

reality of astral influences, while denying that they can have any power over the intellect. On the other hand, such influences can be uncritically accepted when the personality is not awake to its essential possibilities:

> a man might choose naturally to have his operations go on, just as brutes are involved in operations by natural instinct, and as inanimate bodies are moved naturally. In that case there would not be choice and nature, as two active principles, but only one, and that is nature.[6]

He goes on to say that Fate is an order which is inherent in physical things, while Providence is an order which is impressed on them subsequently. To conclude, he says that according to the above meaning, to deny Fate is to deny Providence.[7]

For all the customary avoidance of the word 'Fate' because of its pagan associations, one can see that Aquinas' conception closely corresponds to that of the Neoplatonists. Insofar as the will is subservient to sensation and passion, it is assimilated to a system of forces which take no account of the value or purpose of individuals, but on the contrary uses them in the manner of raw material for the making of new ones which in turn are produced, used, destroyed, and recycled with equal indifference.

The working of physical necessity is more likely to conflict with our personal wellbeing the more we are subject to such necessity, which appears where one is subject to chance events or accidents, since everything related to matter exists at the expense of, or to the exclusion of, something else of like nature. 'Fatal' events of this kind are notably absent from what Scripture and other traditional texts relate of individuals who exemplify providential action in history, and it is also noteworthy that the word 'accident' has only acquired the meaning it has today during the last three hundred years, during which reality has become more and more equated with materiality and Fate.

6. *SCG*, III, chap. 85, [4].
7. Ibid., chap. 93, [5–6].

The apparent paradox of 'escaping Fate' has already been discussed in connection with free will. While it cannot be escaped physically, it can be escaped in a more essential manner which reduces its determining influence over the person to a subordinate position. This involves the familiar duality of spirit and matter and the soul's position in relation to them. The soul's salvation, or positive relation to Providence, depends on which of these two orientations has the determining influence on it. In other words, man has in a certain sense to create his own identity, whether it be on the level of value or on that of the sense world for its own sake, normally over a long period of assimilation to the one or the other.

The biggest difficulty raised by this is that it can be mistaken for an attempt to negate the material creation as such, whereas the material level of being is universally necessary to complete the total range of being, that is, the Great Chain of Being. A supposed spirituality which would negate it is therefore a futile attempt to limit reality to what some human beings think they want. Conversely, the materialistic option is an equally futile attempt to give the most dependent and most unstable parts of the Chain of Being a total reality to the exclusion of the higher members of it on which they depend. Losing the latter, this must ultimately result in the loss of the former as well. Conversely, the true way retains both.

These principles have a fundamental importance for the way in which we understand history. Providence, as particular providence, is a universal element in the religions which have shaped history. Many historical events have been brought about by those whose wills were joined to Providence, and many others by wills that were Fate-bound. Where the latter are predominant, the results are states of conflict and disorder which often merge with disasters of a natural kind before order is restored. The opposed forces can appear more or less equal in strength, but it is not the same kind of strength. The one contains the principle of universal order by affiliation to God, while the other has endless possibilities of disrupting the true order because of the way its action proceeds from inadequate and inferior causes.

This ensures the ultimate success of those who identify with Providence, as reality must comprise order and in the last analysis there is only one order. There are besides acts of Divine intervention which were always believed in before people started to believe in accidents and blind chance. According to the historian quoted before:

> the belief that our world is governed by isolated acts of Divine intervention, and that in consequence every great calamity, whether physical, military, or political, may be regarded as a punishment or a warning, was the basis of the whole religious system of antiquity.[8]

This continued directly from pagan religion to Christianity, not by imitation, but because of the very nature of theistic religion and the belief that man is free to will in accordance with the ultimate cause of the world or to defy it. According to early Christian histories, the victory by which Constantine became the first Christian emperor, and the sudden death of Arius were clear proofs of the truth of the orthodox faith and the falsehood of Arianism. Even the fall of the Roman Empire did not shake this idea of particular providence, except that the idea of vindication by temporal success became confined to that of the Church as a spiritual power rather than as a worldly one. Modern religion has retreated from this point of view, owing to embarrassments about 'historicism' and a supposed need to be 'non-judgmental', without facing the fact that the alternative is a tacit Deism or even complete unbelief.

When collective revolts against the providential order occur, they are essentially so much defiance of the cause of their own existence. Nevertheless, the destructive forces come not from God or Providence itself, but from the very power which is misused and made into a kind of god. No violent or destructive action ever comes directly from God,[9] but because of ignorance of this, the idea of Divine retribution is misunderstood as meaning some malevolence in God, and made into an excuse for a new complaint against the truth was in any case being ignored. Because of this incomprehension, modern thought is mostly committed to the belief that history has

---

8. W. E. H. Lecky, *A History of European Morals*, bk. 1, chap. 3.
9. See Aquinas, *SCG*, 1, chap. 19.

been a tale of meaningless disasters and privations except where it contained the causes of today's world. This is because it is assumed that only applied science and political intervention are able to set a limit to human and natural evils. Such conclusions follow from the usual question-begging circle of materialistic premises.

It is normally assumed today that the world is not able adequately to support human life without increasingly radical interferences with natural processes, because there is no recognition that this need for changing the course of nature results mostly from the ways in which mankind relates unspiritually to the world. The human race does not see itself as a member of a hierarchy of being, but merely as an isolated force dominating as many other forces as possible. The natural evils of life are therefore thought to be meaningless, resulting only from a lack of preventive technique. This is supported by a race memory that human destiny includes a rulership over nature, but this is misunderstood in purely physical terms. A state of wellbeing which has been rightly described as the prerogative of spiritual athletes[10] is thus presumed to be a right for absolutely everyone.

Accordingly, the Fate-governed realm, normally dangerous and treacherous, has been made artificially safe, such that the distinction between wisdom and folly would seem to be an irrelevance. The creation of a literal 'fool's paradise' in which the true principle of life can be ignored is in any case an inevitable result of an artificial and uprooted intelligence. Nevertheless, the ancient dangers are as real as ever, because the Law of Action and Reaction is not annulled by increases in purely physical power over cosmic conditions, even though reactions can thereby be delayed.

Attempts to suppress the operation of the Law are liable to bring about so much the greater ultimate reaction in proportion to the length of time it has been held off. Ample warning on this point has been given by the two World Wars, though in fact they have only accelerated the tendencies which brought them about. Modern history has, on its negative side, been a continuous attempt to liberate mankind from Providence on the one hand, and its implication that we are in this world for a purpose not of our own choosing, and at

10. Stephen Clark, *Civil Peace and Sacred Order.*

the same time to liberate it from the rogue forces of Fate which would naturally follow from this. If this succeeded in the long term, mankind would have succeeded in opting out of its place in the cosmic hierarchy, while retaining a dominance over nature based on human powers and techniques alone. Nothing further from truth and stability could be conceived, nor anything better calculated to result in a stampede into the jaws of Fate in its most inhuman form.

Blindness to such realities is deeply associated with a denial of the doctrine of Original Sin. The ego is centered on a determination to be itself and nothing else, regardless of meaning or value, and this passion is now freed from all restraints. Human beings therefore believe themselves to be all born essentially good, and this has the consequence that the source of all evils must be found everywhere and anywhere except in ourselves, which is a good example of the 'projection' which psychology finds in sick minds. Joseph de Maistre is far nearer the truth where he says that 'there is no human evil which is not the result of some sin forbidden by Scripture.'

This point of view emphasizes the sufficiency of Providence for human wellbeing and the irrelevance of pretended alternatives, but it demands a love of truth and of God which must be greater than the natural love of one's own ego. A certain kind energy is needed for this, one which old civilizations fail to retain or cultivate, when instead they identify with their 'fatal' condition.

FATE AND ASTROLOGY

The modern preoccupation with astrology is an entirely natural result of a collective identification Fate which is not recognized for what it is. From what has been argued already, it is not difficult to show both why astrology is based on valid principles and why it should not be made a rule of life.

The effective predictive power of astrology for any given person must be in proportion to his or her identification with Fate in its individual form, that is, insofar as the individual will reflects heredity and early environment. Much depends on the extent to which such things affect the will consciously or not. On the one hand, a detailed knowledge of the determining forces to which one is subject can open the way to a new freedom, since the most dangerous influences are the ones which operate unnoticed. On the other hand, if these influences are accepted as though they had prescriptive rights over the person, they can bar the way to moral and intellectual maturity and full individuation. But with assimilation to Providence and free will, the goods and evils which result from the interactions of Fate cease to be a central issue. In this case, one will act in a certain way because it is known to be right, and not because of possible rewards and penalties.

Apart from questions of self-interest, however, life would be lacking in a dimension if there was no awareness of its connections to the movements of the cosmos. The real world is an organic whole, not a collection of mechanical accidents, and each individual is in truth the center of an immense sphere of influences. The interactions involved are subject to the Law of Cosmic Sympathy, by which all beings are joined by qualitative likenesses. This extends to the correspondences between individuals and the states of their world as it was at the time of their birth. Such correspondences are as natural as the way in which the quality of a wine reflects that of its year.

Besides their metaphysical basis, such ideas are supported by scientific discoveries about the ways in which the Solar System varies the strength of the earth's magnetic field, and the ways in which living organisms respond to magnetic forces. But more is involved than the pulsations of cosmic energies, because the other major factor is that of timing. Those which act at the beginning of a life have a special kind of power, in accordance with the principle that the nature of the first member of a series determines that of all those that follow from it. The later members of the series can never get free from the original one, because the production of each one is always more or less an extension of the causality of the first. This is expressed in the maxim that the end of every undertaking may be discovered by the face of the heavens at the time it begins.

Though no one has power over the determinations Fate puts upon them, such things dictate only the starting-points whence free action can develop. Whereas all beings are 'sown' in the world as creatures of Fate, the purpose of life is to develop from this to free will and individuation. This can be helped by a deeper understanding of one's origins. Despite the dubious uses often made of it, astrology belongs by right to any traditional body of knowledge. It shows in terms of an individual life the universal principle that the nature of the whole is manifest in the part, where its parts are ensouled beings with their unique world-representations.

Its general implication that human lives are linked with their world by being qualified by a common set of archetypes is also an idea which follows from the principles of Neoplatonism. Although there is an order of pure necessity, it is not necessary that any given individual should identify with it or be subject to it. Because necessity is conditional, freedom is possible.

13

THE DIRECTION
OF THE VITAL FORCE

MORALITY AND CULTURE

The distinction between Fate and Providence means that the will does not act so much on the world so much as on two interpenetrating parts of the world. These realities differ profoundly, despite being completely mingled in the world, and yet they are separable by the prioritizations which mankind makes between them. The pressure to incline one way or another comes from the fact that all human energies are strictly limited, so that their development in any one direction inevitably means their withdrawal from other directions. The typical 'pagan' outlook ignores this truth and takes the person to be an unlimited resource that can be spread everywhere.

Some such insight underlies traditional moral codes, especially where sexual morality is concerned, where it was integrated with their metaphysical knowledge. It is not now considered appropriate to treat morality from a theoretical point of view, because knowledge is equated with immediate experience, owing to a distrust of the intellect. But for those who are willing to see that sexual behavior does not exist in a magical isolation from everything else, there have been modern sources of insight, one of which was discussed by Aldous Huxley in relation to the history of culture.

A good point of departure for the present subject is Huxley's summary of Dr. J.D Unwin's researches,[1] which explore the relationship between the intellectual and creative energies of cultures

1. J.D. Unwin, *Sex and Culture*.

and their differing degrees of sexual freedom. The lowest cultural level among those he studied, which he calls the 'zoistic', has the lowest levels of moral restraint:

> Investigation shows that the societies exhibiting the least amount of energy are those where pre-nuptial continence is not imposed and where opportunities for sexual indulgence are greatest. The cultural condition of a society rises in exact proportion as it imposes prenuptial and post-nuptial restraints upon sexual opportunity.[2]

This kind of restraint is typically that of societies with a strong commitment to monogamous values. The resulting state of such societies can be seen from history in their having the surplus energy for many things, including colonial expansion, as well as creativity in the arts and sciences. Examples of this can be seen in ancient Greece in the seventh and sixth centuries BC, and in Europe in the eighteenth and nineteenth centuries. There is an entropy law involved in this, by which energy is not created or absolutely lost, but can either be concentrated and made to work, or be dissipated into ever smaller and less creative amounts.

History also shows that where the relaxation of moral restraints in society in general is resisted by minorities within it, those minorities acquire a higher level of energy than the rest of society and so rise to privileged and dominant positions in it. This is illustrated by the rise of the Christians in the Roman Empire, where many of the highest positions under the Emperor were held by Christians even before the reign of Constantine, when they were still only about ten percent of the population. Similarly, the Jews achieved a position in European culture and economic life out of all proportion to their numbers, and here again they are a minority which places a high value on monogamous marriage and the family

It appears that the relaxation of moral values over long periods has resulted in both social classes and whole nations becoming subordinated to others, as their conscious unity dissolves (surplus energy and consciousness are inseparable). For some minds, this

2. Huxley, *Ends and Means*, chap. 15.

picture is obscured by the fact that high forms of culture can usually continue for at least another generation after traditional moral restraints have given way, creating the impression that a society can have the best of both worlds. In this connection, Huxley points out that the most creative periods in history do not last very long, the reason being that voluntary self-restraint is too much of a burden for human nature. No civilized society as a whole is willing to accept the reduction of sexual opportunity to a minimum for very long. This is because of a failure to see any meaning in it beyond the worldly practicalities involved.

However, the distribution of available energies, important as it is, is still not the basic principle here. Restrictive sexual morality, chastity, and celibacy cannot be understood on a merely cultural basis because there are no adequate humanistic reasons for them. Instead, these things arise from possibilities which belong to the esoteric, in the light of which alone they can be understood. It is a sign of the corruption of today's world that, even where the esoteric is written about, nothing is said about the meaning of a morality which has nothing to do with social utility. Without knowledge of such things, attempts to transform the inner nature of life will end in self-delusion. To try to realize all possibilities on all levels is merely a form of self-destruction, besides being an evasion of hard decisions. A decision between two sets of priorities is forced on mankind by its psycho-physical constitution, which I will illustrate with some texts of Plato.

The deeper meaning of Plato's cosmology has been observed by Simone Weil,[3] where she sees the image of man as a plant with its roots in the heavens as an expression of a theory of chastity. The account Plato gives of it is hard to follow, because it has been written without a clear sequence of ideas. This inverted plant is watered by 'a celestial water', or 'a divine semen', which is received by the head, which is the real 'root' of the person. When man is consciously open to this influence and cooperates with it, he cultivates the spiritual and intellective part of himself, but if he fails to do so, the energy in question is not lost, but assumes a different form. In Plato's terms, it

3. Simone Weil, *Intimations of Christianity*, chap. 8.

descends from the brain, down through the spinal column, until it ends up as carnal desire.

The implication of this is that carnal desire is a secondary or derivative thing, a materialized imitation of the love of God. This point of view is the exact opposite of the modern idea that physical sexuality is the central reality and that love of God is a sublimation of it. It is in accordance with the archetypalist conception that it is the intelligible reality which is both the pattern and productive cause of physical reality. Since the relevant texts can easily seem to be about nothing more than an outdated form of natural science, besides being presented in an order which obscures their meaning, I shall quote them at length in a different order which will make their concealed meaning clearer.

ESOTERIC MORALITY IN PLATO

Where Plato uses the word 'marrow', it refers to the most essential material of the body, regardless of where in the body it is said to reside. This substance is specially sensitive to the interaction of soul and body, and is formed from the principles of all four elements:

> Mixing these in due proportion to one another, he (the Demiurge) fashioned therefrom the marrow, contriving thus a compound of seeds of every sort for every mortal kind. Next he implanted and tied therein the various kinds of souls (of men and of beasts); also from the outset, while making his original distribution, he divided the marrow into shapes corresponding in number and fashion to those which the several kinds were destined to wear. *And he moulded into spherical shape the ploughland, so to speak, that was to contain the divine seed; and this part of the marrow he called 'brain',* signifying that, when each living creature was completed, the vessel containing this should be the head. That part, however, which was to contain the remaining (mortal) kind of soul he divided into shapes at once rounded and elongated, naming them all 'marrow'.[4]

4. Plato, *Timaeus*, 73 C, D, Warrington translation.

All mindless passion is said to be related to excesses and disorders in the 'marrow', with these two things acting reciprocally on one another:

> When a man suffers transports of joy or torments of pain, he is frenzied, and his capacity for reasoning is then at its lowest ebb. Moreover, when the seed in a man's marrow becomes super-charged with moisture, like a tree carrying too much fruit, he is filled on each occasion with intense agony and with pleasure equally intense, both in his desires and in his satisfaction. For most of his life he is maddened by these strong pleasures and pains; and when the body renders his soul sick and senseless he is commonly considered to be not sick, but deliberately wicked. But the truth is that sexual intemperance is a disease of the soul, arising largely from the condition of a single substance (the mar-row) which, owing to the porosity of the bones, floods the body with its moisture.[5]

> Hence it was at that time that the gods contrived the craving for sexual intercourse, fashioning one animate creature in us males, and another in women. The two were made by them in the fol-lowing way. From the conduit of our drink, where it receives liq-uid that has passed into the bladder and ejects it with the air that presses on it, they pierced a hole giving access to the compact marrow *which runs from the head down the neck and along the spine* and has in fact, earlier in this discourse been termed 'seed'. This marrow, being instinct with life and finding an outlet implanted in the part occupied by this outlet a keen appetite for egress and so brought it to completion as an Eros of begetting until at length the Eros of the one and the Desire of the other bring the pair (man and woman) together, pluck as it were *the fruit of the tree and sow the plough land of the womb* with living creatures still unformed and so small as to be invisible. . . .[6]

These texts give an account of the natural condition of mankind,

5. Ibid., 86 C, D.
6. Ibid., 91 A, B, D.

but there is no intention of suggesting that it rules by necessity. The first line put in italics shows that the spinal column is taken to be the physical link between the brain and the sex organs, besides which it is said to contain a substance, 'marrow' which is common to both of them. The reference to the 'ploughland of the womb' clearly corresponds to the spherical 'ploughland' of the 'brain' referred to in the previous passage. Both intellectual and sexual functions thus have their corresponding centers in which the common 'seed' or 'marrow' functions in different ways, though the will can determine which of the two will be the dominant one; there is no suggestion that either alone can overrule the other. Thought and will can therefore determine the prevailing direction of the psycho-physical force, which in the above text is toward the sense world. Plato then goes on to say what happens if the 'marrow' moves in the contrary direction, from the sexual center towards the head:

As regards the supreme form of soul in us, we must conceive that the god has conferred it upon each man as a guiding genius - that which we say dwells in the highest part of our body and lifts us from earth toward our celestial affinity, *like a plant whose roots are not in earth, but in the heavens.* And this is most true, for it is to the heavens, whence the soul first came to birth, that the divine part attaches *the head or root of us* and thereby keeps the whole body erect. Now if a man is entirely dedicated to appetites and ambitions and devotes all his energies to these, all his thoughts must needs be mortal, and he cannot help but become altogether mortal (so far as that is possible) since he has fostered the growth of his mortality. If, however, he has set his heart upon learning and true wisdom, and has exercised that part of himself above all others, he is surely bound to think thoughts immortal and divine, if he lay hold on truth; nor can he fail to possess immortality in the fullest measure that human nature allows. And inasmuch as he is forever cherishing the divine part and tending the guardian genius that dwells within him in good estate, he must needs be superlatively happy.[7]

7. Ibid., 90 A, B, C.

Some highly significant equivalences are made in these texts, among the different subtle components of the human constitution united under the term 'marrow,' which has the sense of 'essential substance.' In particular the contents of the brain and the spinal column and the sexual secretions are all treated as being of the same nature, the so-called marrow. The fact that this is not true as biology does not matter here, because Plato is not trying to discuss biology as such. He is using aspects of biology along with a creation myth to explain the spiritual meanings of the relation between soul and body.

There is both an opposition and a complementarism between the 'divine seed' which is received in the 'ploughland' of the brain, and the natural seed which is said to come from the descent of the 'marrow' down the spinal column to the other 'ploughland' of the womb. At the same time, the tree with its roots in the heavens is the counterpart of the overladen tree representing sexual desire. Essentially the same force is involved, but it is one which can be used on two different levels which communicate by means of the spine. The direction of thought and the upward and downward pressures of the 'marrow' act and react on one another reciprocally, and the balance between them, or the lack of it, results in deeply different kinds of lives.

The preference for inward and intellectual experience belongs with the maintenance of psychical energy close to its source, and this has the effect of assimilating the whole person to his spiritual 'root' inasmuch as the brain is in some sort a microcosm of the whole person. Conversely, the captivity of thought and will by material things for their own sake is the counterpart of an uncontrolled descent of the same energy, so that it can only be deployed on the physical level. This assimilates the person as a whole to the natural and corruptible elements of the self, which is also the one which is subject to all manner of external forces. It would follow from the Law of Action and Reaction that the voluntary projection of the self into the material realm must lead to a corresponding projection of the material world into the self, though this does not mean that the alternative to this must put the self out of relation to the world. Rather it is a question as to the exact manner in which the self is in the world.

In the former case, the self is integrated with the world in an unfree manner which involves a mingling of identities between the self and the external world. In the latter case, on the other hand, the self is integrated with its world by a close relationship between the most subtle parts of the self and of the world, which allows both freedom and a certain power at once, two things which would conflict on the purely natural level.

SOME MORAL IMPLICATIONS

While the physiological relations just described are predominantly symbolical by nature, there is also a core of physical truth in them. The fact that the word 'marrow' is used loosely to include a number of substances which are not the same for biology does not mean that the thinking behind it is confused by appearances. Modern studies of the chemical composition of the brain and of the seminal fluid have in fact revealed important similarities between them of a kind which could not have been known in Plato's time. Both are rich in sodium, phosphorus, chlorine, and magnesium, and this means that the brain and the sex organs not only have a chemistry in common, but that they compete with one another for the same substances from the body's supplies. This adds factual reinforcement to the basic intuition that there are here different outlets for the same general kind of energy, which in the extreme case can even be mutually exclusive.

This brings to the fore the relation between intellectuality and morality and their effect on the meaning of life. Far from the intellectual awakening of the soul to a life of its own being merely a matter of taste, or a passion for any kind of knowledge for its own sake, it is the conscious manifestation of a quasi-alchemical function which involves the whole person. Although Plato does not say so directly, the implicit conclusion is drawn by Simone Weil that the uncontrolled descent of the vital force is prevented by the cultivation of its intellective capacities. The dedication of energies in the 'inward' dimension would therefore be a normal response to grace, besides being a means whereby the immortality of the soul is gradually made a matter of direct intuition.

While the soul is essentially separable from the body, its activity still has to be trained so as to realize this essential nature, failing which, it would be immortal in a state of unnatural dependence on material conditions which would involve it in a deep inner conflict. For this reason the immortality of the soul in a personally meaningful sense would be something which has to be achieved through an irreversible process, comparable to the firing of pottery or the baking of bread. This is bound to involve a moral tension which could not be compatible with glib theories of self-integration without dualism and purely natural balance, which are really unspiritual, and treat restraint as unnatural, as though our destiny was wholly confined to the physical level.

This also has a bearing on the effectiveness of what we do in the world, since effective action depends as much on a harmonious relation to the world as upon our direct efforts. There is a kind of disengagement of the self from the world which increases one's power over it, which was referred to before in connection with Providence. While it is beyond human powers to overcome all obstacles, the realistic option is to live in a manner which places one beyond the reach of their most harmful effects. Such is the power of the 'lived truth,' and it is the only form of power which is wholly compatible with freedom and moral goodness.

Whether this ideal is best realized in a married or in a celibate life depends on the individual, and on his place in society. In either case, there are compensating factors, because the stabilization of the vital force at its 'root' is not the same thing as a practice of sexual repression, although it does explain how that kind of morality came into being. Beyond doubt it had been prepared by a long period during which Christian morality was observed in a perfunctory manner, with no one making any effort to understand it in depth. The universal power of love was admitted without thought of the consequence that it must therefore extend far beyond sexuality.

Another major consequence of the esoteric conception is that no desire can be strong of itself, because whatever strength it has could come solely from the frequency with which it is gratified. This inverts the common sense belief that a desire is frequently gratified because it is strong, and the difference here is fundamental, whether in regard to desires of the 'ascending' or the 'descending' movements. The potential for conflict between these two opposite directions of the vital force always remains, and this means that their relationship can be either hierarchical or anarchical, and this inward order or disorder will decide whether the life in the outside world rules the flow of natural forces or is ruled by it.

14

COMPLEXITIES IN
THE IDEA OF GRACE

A CONSEQUENCE OF DEPENDENCE

The teaching that grace is necessary for all good purposes is a corrective to the tendency in human nature to ignore the ways in which it is dependent. That mankind is dependent on grace is affirmed in the face of undoubted experiences of self-reliance, which are always deceptive because the power to will does not include the will to use it. Those who fail to be saints do so only because of a failure to turn their wills in the appropriate direction. Besides, some things really depend on grace when they are mistaken for natural attributes; for example, people often think their love of truth or of freedom are natural to them, but in reality the natural person does not love either truth or freedom.

Nevertheless, I shall not confine the present subject to a straightforward endorsement of the orthodox position, because the full consequences of the need for grace include things which can appear strange or paradoxical from an orthodox point of view. There is a certain realm of self-power which is part of our essence, where being and knowing are one, and from whence the intellect is involved in the conduct of life. F. Schuon has highlighted this issue by means of the idea that, if grace is necessary, intellectuality must be a grace, and that if intellectuality were not a grace, grace would not be necessary.

Taken together with what was said earlier as to how the intelligence is common to both the natural and the supernatural, this means that it cannot be self-contradictory to say that human beings can acquire grace in non-sacramental ways if they have received grace in the first place by the usual means. 'Self-salvation', though self-contradictory in the absence of grace, is in fact just the kind of thing one should expect from those with grace. Otherwise one would be absurdly defending grace on the premise that the only result of receiving it would be a need to receive it again. What is received can in some sense become self-multiplying, or else there would not be much meaning in the Parable of the Sower and the different kinds of soil on which the seed of grace was sown. Dependence itself can have different meanings, as we may be dependent on grace as our presence indoors depends on a door being unlocked, or as the mortally ill depend on life-support systems.

It is possible to understand grace on at least three different levels, the first and most basic of which is in fact just sound realism, the acknowledgement that we are not our own creators, so that what we achieve is to the honour of the Author of our being and not of ourselves alone. Our faculties as well as our being have also their own measure of dependence, since all the actions instigated by our wills require the co-operation of innumerable other forces within us and around us, most of which we know nothing about. Such is the uncontroversial 'ground floor' or 'Level 1' of this conception.

A more particular idea of grace is to be found in the idea that sincere effort can attract the help of providential power which eventually enables it to go far beyond what one's natural strength could have managed. The old adage about those who 'help themselves' reveals a universal awareness of this aspect of grace. This also expresses the law of Cosmic Sympathy by which like attracts like, in this case these being God and those who try to act according to God's will. It should be noted that grace in this realm is in a sense 'earned,' despite the apparent contradiction in this. But the fact that it is given freely is not the same as saying that it must be given to absolutely anyone; there must always be a correspondence between the receiver and the received, as in accordance with the law of Action and Reaction. This idea of grace is not separate from the metaphysical and magical principle of attraction. It goes beyond the basic position that existence and life itself are a grace, whence it may be referred to as the 'Level 2' of this idea.

This idea of grace is also evangelical, since the Parable about the

Talents includes the idea that man's contribution is crowned by God's, with the words 'To him that hath shalt be given,' and the same point is made by Plotinus from the negative standpoint where he says that 'Not even a god could have the right to strike a blow for the unwarlike.' Far-Eastern tradition bears witness to the universality of the same conception in the Taoist story in Lieh Tzu about the aged farmer, Mister Simple of North Mountain, who sets about removing two mountains which blocked access to his land, using nothing more than hand tools. He persisted in the face of ridicule, saying:

> My descendents will go on for ever, but the mountains will get no bigger. Why should there be any difficulty in levelling it? . . . The mountain spirits which carry snakes in their hands heard about it and were afraid he would not give up. They reported it to God, who was moved by his sincerity, and commanded the two sons of K'ua-erh. to carry the mountains on their backs and put one in Shuo-tung, the other in Yung-nan. Since this time there has been no high ground from Chichou in the North to the South bank of the Han river.[1]

No better illustration of the faith which 'moves mountains' could ever be needed. The sincere will is a subtle kind of power which can attract a greater power of a more openly manifest kind.

GRACE OR REMOTE CONTROL?

Nevertheless it is not possible to leave this idea within the above limits. There is a further conception, which may be called 'Level 3,' according to which humans cannot exert their wills for any good purpose unless their wills are acted on specially by grace in their very mode of operation. This inadequacy of the will would follow from the Augustinian idea that the sin of Adam and Eve is transmitted genetically to every generation as part of their essential being, which it rules unopposed, such that without Divine intervention human beings could only sin. (This has to subsist with the equally

1. *Lieh Tzu*, chap.5, 'The Questions of Tang' (A.C. Graham, tr.).

orthodox position that God will not allow even the smallest inter-ference with anyone's free will in order to prevent evil). This extreme view of the Fall implies that the merits of all morally good actions must belong to God who is their real agent.

Taken literally, this would mean that our natural idea of the will was mistaken, and that what we take for the most purely active part of the personality would in fact be passive, since it could not act without God's operation of a kind of control button to which the will has no access for itself. It should be noted in passing that the will's apparent need for particular modifications by grace does not follow from the admission that the will is a created entity. A self-motive created being is just as much a possibility as an alter-motive one. Neither is the Level 3 idea necessary for the Level 2 one, because the latter assumes a will which is free to be self-motive, however inadequately.

Another problem with the Level 3 idea is that the transfer of the merit of human good actions to God does not entail a correspond-ing transfer of the demerit of their bad actions to the devil. On the contrary, the evils done by human beings are held to be truly their own work. There is never supposed to be any *influxus mysticus* to relieve us of the responsibility for sin, and yet it is one and the same will which executes actions which are good, bad, and indifferent. Rationally, it must seem that either both our merits and demerits should be imputed to higher powers of good and evil equally, or that these merits and demerits should both be our own.

If there is a need for special divine interventions in the will in the case of good actions only, it will be hard to draw the line between such cases and those where the actions were morally indifferent. In the extreme case, the Level 3 idea would imply Monistic Pantheism, with its idea that there can be only one real agent, but needless to say, this is not the accepted conclusion. Everything depends on the means by which the will is acted on. For example it can be acted on in a non-physical way by knowledge of right and wrong; this could in a certain sense be said to determine it even in its actual operation. The idea of a joint physical agency is in any case irrelevant. No one doubts that food, water, alcohol, and medicines produce effects by their inherent powers alone. God does not have to intervene to make them produce their effects, and neither is this necessary for human voluntary agency. In the latter case, God can act much more effectively by a *moral* causality.

This can be seen if the Level 3 idea is analyzed into a process of four parts as follows:

1) God wills good actions.

2) You have performed a good action.

3) Therefore God willed your action.

4) Therefore God is the author of your action.

Part 4 of the above follows because, in terms of moral causality, if a person A performs an action because he believes that a person B wants him to do so, B is the real author of the action. Such is the non-physical basis for the Level 3 idea of grace. But because of ignorance of the above idea of moral causes, the Level 3 idea has caused dire confusion in minds which think only in terms of physical causes and the logic that applies to them, and the problem resulting from this became the central issue of the Reformation. Martin Luther's most influential book, *The Bondage of the Will*, is a root-and-branch denial of free will, based on unshakeably Christian sources. Free will was not found to be affirmed in any of the sources of revelation; God alone was the agent, at least in any literal reading. Paradoxically, the resulting conclusion that man's will was in no way free from God's control (misunderstood as a kind of physical control), was in fact just as liberating as an unqualified affirmation of free will would have been.

This was because Catholic doctrine did not endorse either of the obvious alternatives, and the resulting position was defined by the tension between them. If, on the other hand, man was so unfree that he had to be given grace by a special act of God before he could do anything good, there would be no point in Church authorities trying to tell people what to do, and in this case obedience would not have any meaning or use. Either God would operate their controls and they would do the right thing, or He would not, and they would not. Thus while man was therefore in theory a slave to God's will, the simplification involved meant that he was free to live without moral tension on his own level; there was thus a new kind of wholeness, won at the price of perfectibility.

Before this, free will was affirmed selectively, as in cases where obedience or acknowledgement of guilt was requisite, while denying it in the case of actions which were liable to reflect credit on those who performed them. In the latter, the agency was assigned to God. This treatment of grace and free will is effectual from a devotional point of view, if not from a philosophical one, because it excludes man's naturalistic equilibrium by systematically marginalizing the claims of the ego. But because free will was not a specifically Christian teaching, the Reformers thought it should be removed for the sake of a purified Christian message. However, they did not realize that the penalty for this was to be a new kind of spiritual neutralism.

TWO SOURCES OF TRUTH

Ideas about man's dependence on grace are further confused because of the duality in human nature, between its physical or observable self and its soul or 'greater self'. These levels of selfhood are not necessarily integrated, and their spiritual needs cannot be the same. In the one case, grace must come in socially and historically determined forms, whereas in the other, it will be individual and non-historical. Orthodox teachings which deny possibility of grace except through sacred tradition and its consecrated ministers are justified, as long as it is understood that this applies to the direct reception of historically-determined grace. It does not apply to grace which has spread laterally, so to speak, from sacred tradition, and neither does it apply to a grace which comes through an awakening of the intellect.

Such an awakening is implicit in nearly all of those who are moved to seek God, and they are either moved by the Holy Spirit or they are not. If they are, they confirm the existence of a non-historical or 'gnostic' grace. If, on the other hand, this were not so, it could only mean that grace was not necessary, at least for them. In orthodox terms, any movement toward God is by definition the work of the Holy Spirit, and so from this point of view it would be safer to argue that it is really a matter of definition: grace received through a historical, revealed religion cannot be the same as grace from a non-historical source. Put this way, it need not involve claims for an exclusive truth for either metaphysical or revealed religion, and still less for any exclusion of the one by the other.

We may thus reach the unforced conclusion that grace can be obtained by different means which cannot be confounded with one another, and neither of which need be self-sufficient for any one person. This would not require any unprovable theories as to whether either the historical or the non-historical kind of grace could suffice for salvation without the other. In real life, there is no means of actually separating them, because no one is ever able to begin their life anywhere where the two are not mingled. Besides, in the life of any person these two sources of grace continually feed and confirm one another. Without the non-historical or indigenous grace, the historically revealed kind would be without effect, having nothing to interact with in the individual soul. Conversely, without a source of grace grounded in the regular, objective conditions of life, the interior kind usually dwindles down to a mere potentiality, for lack of anything to activate it. But the idea that the latter is exclusively necessary is inseparable from the belief that the real self is the ego and nothing else. This belief was criticized in chapter 1, and with it the idea that the whole self can be comprehended in a set of external relations.

The orthodoxy of this dual nature of grace can be seen clearly enough from the fact that it is reflected in the principle on which Scholastic philosophy is based, namely, that we obtain the truth from reason and Revelation equally. These sources of grace must be integrated, and can only fail to be so in a personality which is itself not integrated. In such cases, the results would be either those of activity without truth, or truth without activity, that is to say, without a way of life that reflects it.

These considerations leave wide open the question as to what proportions these two sources of grace should bear to one another in any given individual. While a combination of both may well be necessary for everyone, some may need both equally, while yet others may need much more of the one than the other, and there should be no question of praise or blame for those who differ from the average in such ways.

The desire to pass over or minimize the indigenous intellective form of grace can be seen to lead to a kind of thinking which presents itself as definitive in a way which does not quite conceal a certain incoherence, even in writings which are otherwise enlightening. In one instance, it occurs in the writings of Thomas Merton:

> And so the true contemplative life does not consist in the enjoyment of spiritual and interior pleasures. Contemplation is something more than a refined and holy aestheticism of the intellect and will, in love and faith. To rest in the beauty of God as a pure concept, without the accidents of image or sensible species or any other representation, is a pleasure which still belongs to the human order. It is perhaps the highest pleasure to which nature has access and many people do not arrive at it by their natural powers alone—they need grace before they can experience the satisfaction which is of itself within the reach of nature. And nevertheless, since it is natural, and can be desired by nature and acquired by natural disciplines, it must not be confused with supernatural contemplation. True contemplation is a work of love that transcends all satisfaction and all experience to rest in the night of pure and naked faith.[2]

Here, the difference between objective and subjective states is not considered at all. The key words used are those which designate Nature, Pleasure, the Human, Faith, Work, Grace, and the Supernatural. The references to nature emphasize its spiritual deficiencies, which would be reasonable enough if the supernatural were made known by something more than the emotional states linked to apparently natural conditions by which it is referred to here. A further instance of the same tendency is the identification of truth with things which are at least apparently natural, such as the painful or a severe effort of will, and likewise there are further references to the transcendent by way of natural *accidentalia* such as Work, Love, Night, and Rest. Such terms do not, apparently, take us any distance from the natural level which is never fully spiritual.

---

2. Thomas Merton, *Seeds of Contemplation*, chap. 28.

It is also curious that Merton should think it an argument against what he takes to be the lower kind of contemplation that it can be 'acquired by natural disciplines,' when the monastic life itself is based on that very thing. The conviction which this passage carries is largely owing to its evocation of innumerable half-forgotten experiences of the conflict between pleasure and duty. But the fact that this reflects a truth in the realm of practicalities does not mean that it must work as metaphysics. Contemplation on whatever level is not dependent on the relative and transient conditions which shape the impressions referred to in the above, or otherwise it could not reach truth. The question as to how agreeable or otherwise it may be cannot be a means of judging its spirituality because such reactions result primarily from the peculiarities of individuals.

The idea that true contemplation is not as pleasant as the natural kind involves a confusion of accidentals with essentials. According to Aristotle,[3] when we have once really understood spiritual wisdom, all other things are bound to seem unimportant, and this property of the spiritual good cuts across all questions as to the pleasant or the unpleasant; a sense of absolute meaning and value leaves no reason why any level of contemplation should be intrinsically the one or the other.

A more objective distinction between the natural and the supernatural is referred to in the above as that of 'perfect acceptance of God's will,' regardless of our personal feelings about the way things should be. But even in this case, there is no reason why the 'natural' contemplation should not also be God's will, depending on the individuals concerned. If pleasure is not a reliable criterion, then by the same token neither in principle should pain be. But some kinds of spirituality may be only a form of escapism, or as Merton puts it, 'a refuge from the responsibility of suffering in darkness and obscurity and helplessness, allowing God to strip us of our false selves. . . .'[4]

The assumption here is that naturally negative states of being can bring us closer to truth and reality, and there is truth in this inasmuch as we cannot be sure that grace is real unless it can stand the

3. Aristotle, *Protrepticus*, [96],[106]. Anton-Herman Chroust, ed.
4. See *Seeds of Contemplation*, chap. 32.

tests of opposition and suffering. The goal of perfection must include a good which is stronger than all the violence which disordered nature can inflict on it, and such evils will unwittingly enhance our grasp of the truth, as in the idea of transcendence in chapter 7. But this calls for a rather different perspective. Under Providence, the normal course of life brings all the trials necessary for this purpose, without that conferring any value or meaning on suffering for its own sake. It must be remembered that states of suffering are in any case always more likely to result from sinful and foolish rather than from virtuous living; the normative result of living the truth remains a happiness which links the natural with the supernatural.

WILL, GRACE, AND POWER

There is, of course, no mistake in insisting on the objective distinction between the natural and the supernatural, if it is made on an adequate basis. One difference between them can be seen in that between valid thought which is 'about' a given thing in a way which reveals truth, and consciousness and sensation which exist without reference, like physical objects, i.e., the classic distinction between Reason and Nature. While the supernatural includes reason, it extends far beyond it as well, but reason is the most accessible form of it. It is also beyond the limitations of space and time, while having a complexity which can only be manifest in diverse appearances.

In spite of this, the issue gets confused by the fact that revealed religion is based on revelation which takes the form of events in history which, although physical in form, are Divine or supernatural in their essence, and so are themselves recognized as supernatural. As such, they are the exception which proves the rule, since they are necessarily called supernatural, while being the same in form as things which are only natural. From a Platonic point of view, something similar could be said of the creation of the whole universe, but where it is a case of historical revelation, the cosmogonic process is taking place a second time in microcosm, that is, within the world formed by the original outgoing movement.

One unwanted consequence of revelation covering the extremes of the natural and supernatural, like the events of the Incarnation, has been that many minds are misled into ignoring the distinction between these levels of reality. The result can be an unintentional materialism which hinders any clear understanding of theoretical questions. One may give up the attempt to distinguish the natural and the supernatural by intrinsic factors, and simply refer the matter to traditional formulae which are not concerned with the essence of these things as such. Nevertheless, the fact that the supernatural is manifest in historical events makes it more, not less, needful to understand the metaphysical issue involved here.

It would be an inversion of the truth to take the doctrine that God became man to mean that God has somehow endorsed a belief that historical or natural criteria are a more reliable guide to truth than are metaphysical ones. If the workings of the intelligence can be illusions, so also can the contents of sensation, there including the external and visible proofs of religious beliefs. Of the two, it is sensation which is the more liable to error, because, as Schuon puts it, 'phenomena are made for the intelligence, and not the reverse.' Besides, the intelligence can provide proof from itself alone, whereas proof from facts or phenomena depends equally on the mind which identifies them and understands their significance. Pure sensation tells us nothing.

The views quoted from Merton are representative of a tendency of orthodoxy to equate the self with the ego, and therefore with the physical and the phenomenal. Such views can easily conflict with the idea of spiritual enlightenment as an empowerment of the person, because a state of natural impotence can in principle remove barriers between man and God where the individual is spiritually ready for it, whereas a state of natural security or equilibrium can leave one free to follow any false trail unchecked. The issue here is complex because it makes the subjective and the objective hard to separate. On the one hand, the development of self-power in the spiritually immature merely leads to a self-reduction to the ego level. On the other hand, the evil in this is owing to the timing and context of self-power, not to the thing itself.

Power also raises problems if we think as though we were never intended to have it. Although it is true that power resulting from spirituality is not the same as the purely natural kind, that does not mean that the two are mutually exclusive. In reality, they have much in common, however much they differ in their origins. Despite the moral dangers attaching to power of any kind, it remains nevertheless as necessary as knowledge and moral goodness for the realization of the state man was made for. Power is inseparable from both existence and freedom equally, so that it cannot be in any way accidental to the human state.

This can be seen from the nature of existence itself. Everything which exists, even the inorganic, has some degree of causal power; existence entails causality. For living beings, existence and activity are inseparable, while power is simply this innate activity disciplined, concentrated and directed to true values. This connects with freedom, because with freedom, power of this kind works without obstruction, and this in turn is the objective basis of happiness. Thus there are specially close relations between existence, activity, power, freedom and happiness. When it is said that we were created for happiness, this is the way in which it is integrated with the fullness of being. The gift of existence could be compared with the planting of a seed which grows until it produces flowers and fruit in the forms of activity, power, and their consequents.

The main limitation of this analogy is that the growth of a plant or tree is part of the natural order, and so is under most conditions automatic. In the case of the spiritual vocation, on the other hand, the natural or fate-bound condition must be overcome or tamed, because the realm of fate always tries, so to speak, to retain its domination over all who enter life under it. To outside observation, it seems to be a matter of chance whether people remain thus under fate, or whether they escape it. There is a paradox in the fact that the will must collaborate with grace and Providence before it can contend with its fated condition, while it must resist the latter in order to collaborate with Providence. As if in defiance of logic, this miracle never ceases to happen, and when it does, the human will, once joined to Providence, becomes the strongest force in the world, as Fabre d'Olivet eloquently expounds it:

> according to this doctrine, of which sufficiently strong traces can be recognized in Plato, the Will, exerting itself by faith, was able

to subjugate Necessity itself, to command Nature, and to work miracles. Jesus saying parabolically that by means of faith one could remove mountains, only spoke according to the theosophical traditions known to all the sages. 'The uprightness of the heart and faith triumphs over all obstacles,' said Kong-Tse; 'All men can render themselves equal to the sages and the heroes whose memory the nations revere,' said Meng-Tse; 'it is never the power which is lacking, it is the will; provided one desires, one succeeds.' These ideas of the Chinese theosophists are found in the writings of the Indians, and even in those of some Europeans who, as I have already observed, had not enough erudition to be imitators. 'The will which goes resolutely forward is faith; it models its own form in spirit and overcomes all things; by it a soul receives the power of carrying its influence in another soul, and of penetrating its most intimate essences. When it acts with God it can overthrow mountains, break the rocks, confound the plots of the impious, and breathe upon them disorder and dismay . . . all the elect have a similar power. Evil disappears before them. Nothing can harm the one in whom God dwells.'[5]

This passage brings out the implications of what was said before in regard to Providence and Fate as well as what has been said about the true nature of power. Union with Providence means the fullest participation in the Incarnation of Christ. In this ultimate ideal, the human will becomes the third member of the 'Great Triad' (God, Man and Nature), and therefore one of the highest powers.

5. *The Golden Verses of Pythagoras*, chap. 12.

15

GOD AND PHILOSOPHY

PERSONAL AND IMPERSONAL REALITY

Questions of action and reaction, and the choice between physical necessity and a necessity of the rational kind can easily be taken to mean that God is something less than personal, and that creation itself may proceed from God in a way which does not involve any particular concern or attention. Nevertheless, the fact that philosophy always concentrates on universal laws and principles does not necessarily conflict with the orthodox idea of a personal God because the hard alternatives of Individual Person and Universal Principle are not exclusive in the Divine nature, which is the cause of both. Even on the human level, they are by no means wholly exclusive, because the unique individual possesses the universal faculty of reason as part of one and the same being.

There is in any case much in ordinary experience which can show that personal and impersonal realities are really complementary. The freedom of the will, for example, presupposes that the natural order is not free to change itself, so that our freedom can make effectual plans and decisions. When we act freely, moreover, our action is implicitly in accordance with the laws of mechanics, physiology, psychology, and, it may be hoped, with those of reason and morality as well. At the same time, the action can be both free and personally meaningful, so that there is no reason to doubt that such a fusion of personal and impersonal principles also exists in God, as befits the ultimate archetype of our own being. If God was purely impersonal, man would in a real sense be greater than God.

For this reason, the account of human destiny in terms of the Law of Action and Reaction, and the relation between soul and body, together with the direction of the vital force toward the intellect, do not dictate a depersonalized relation to God. These things are rather the universal framework on which a closer assimilation of human nature to the Divine can develop. The unity of the world can in any case be believed in without its being taken to mean that this unity must be comprehensible to human minds. The grand unity of things as diverse as the personal and the impersonal, and of the different traditions, can only be known in its completeness by its Creator.

Consequently, the separate realms of religion, mysticism, philosophy, and science would not necessarily be in conflict, even if human minds could not understand their interaction. But in fact their interaction can to a large extent be understood from the way in which the individual soul or person is a special member of the universal intelligible realities, the Forms. Thus the universal and the individual reside in the same substance. That this is not just a paradox results from the fact that the differing orders of universality in the Forms conclude with a limiting case which can have only one instance, this being the individual soul and the body in which it is instantiated.

The relation between orthodox religion and metaphysics is still no more problematical than between orthodox religion and mysticism. In practice, the great mystics, or at least a majority of them, are accepted without question as part of orthodox tradition. Nevertheless, they challenge the understanding of religion in a specially direct manner. Christian worship is based on a liturgical reliving of the essential events of salvation history, e.g., the Nativity, the Crucifixion, the Resurrection, the Ascension, and many others. In more basic terms, this means that Christian worship consists in constantly driving home the reality of events which happened at particular places and times. But the experience of the mystics, if one can generalize about it at all, is filled with an intuition that particular places and times are not real as such, in which case mysticism could be taken to be deeply heretical, on literal terms at least. It has to be understood that mystical experience lives in the universal content of the events of revelation in a way which overflows the historical means by which we know them.

On a certain level, at least, the incompatibility between mysticism and revealed religion could be insoluble and yet in reality they are nearly always supportive of one another, because the distinction between them follows that of the twofold nature of the true self, in relation to which revealed or historical religion corresponds to its immanent aspect and mysticism to its transcendental aspect. The real world consists of both formal entities, and their causes which transcend physical form, and the human soul can only be satisfied with a view of reality which gives full scope to both.

INDIVIDUATION AND THE IDEAL

Mystical experience is also relevant to the question of spirituality and power, because a greater proximity to God is also a greater proximity to the archetypal principles by which the world is informed. All systems of value are coordinated with one another so that to rise or fall in one of them is implicitly to rise or fall in the others as well, unless there is some intentional obstruction. Values such as the True, the Virtuous, the Beautiful, the Powerful, the Lovable, are thus like the triangular faces of a multisided pyramid. Each position on each one of them implies a corresponding position on the other ones. (If all values are united in God, this convergence is a natural deduction from orthodox beliefs.) Thus a closer relation to the source of creation must include among other things a certain power, even though it be not of a kind which derives from the ego, but rather from the relations in which the ego subsists. Nevertheless, the result is similar enough to personal power for one to be able to speak of it in such terms without much imprecision.

The common dislike of confronting this question is to a large extent sentimental, and when it gets the upper hand it leads to the perverse result that one effectively worships in others the power one denies to oneself, even in its most worldly forms. One's own unworthiness can easily work out as a belief in the worthiness of persons who manifest some kind of power, however undeserving they may be. Something of the historical character of Christianity is attributable to this paradox, which arises where moral asceticism invades rational judgement.

This presence of power among the eternal verities implies that the conditions for the saving of the soul are not too different from those which are necessary for achieving the right kind of power in relation to one's environment so as to thrive or be at least reasonably secure in it. Otherwise, the pursuit of a consistent set of priorities would be impossible. The fact that this idea has been over-worked by some Protestant traditions, with their belief that worldly success proves one's election in Old Testament terms, does not make it any less true in principle. If it were not true, it could only mean that there was an absolute discontinuity between the realms of Nature and Grace, such as would follow from a Manichaen dualism. But in fact Christian and Neoplatonic thought are united in the idea that the natural world corresponds to its Origin, despite its fallen state. It is in accordance with Biblical teachings that what is right and good on the spiritual level must normally be accompanied by corresponding goods on the natural level.

The belief that mankind was created so that it could be happy, both in this life and the next, is hard to refute when it is understood that happiness is the state in which beings exist to the fullest extent possible for them, in which they can act freely. Only in cases where there was a direct conflict between natural and spiritual happiness would this point of view need modification. Happiness cannot be real or lasting except in relation to moral and spiritual truth.

One consequence of this, namely, that a personal autonomy should be part of the ideal, may sound strange, but this is implicit in what was affirmed of human nature in connection with Providence and Fate. The soul relates to the world as a whole because it, unlike lower forms of consciousness, is itself a whole of a kind which corresponds to the wholeness of the world. For this reason, man as such can never be a part in relation to any cosmic reality, and the conscious development of this wholeness is the true purpose of the individuating process.

This element of self-realization is inescapable for the basic physiological reason that the first two decades of nearly every human life consist in that very thing. The transition from birth to the start of adulthood embodies a pattern of activity which is thenceforth a second nature. At the start of life, the mind has to engage with the truth about the world as a whole, whence there is something of the philosopher, the scientist, and the artist in everyone. This is not to ignore the fact that there is much in religious experience which on another level runs counter to the idea of the autonomous individual. There is a spiritual 'putting on Christ' which can easily seem to contradict the values of individuality. But if it did so in a way which did not mean a higher expansion of the individual state, we should be subject to illusion to a degree that would make it pointless to rely on the human mind in any way.

There is a near-instinctive objection to individuality as a value that results from its being seen a *per se* a state of limitation. This objection is constantly supported by evidence from the ever-abundant examples of human individualities who are only too obviously limited. (Plotinus had something like this in mind when he said that no one would ever doubt the immortality of souls were it not for the numerous spoiled souls.) But sickness can never be an argument against health, and in no way can a widespread failure to develop a given possibility be an argument against that possibility itself. The individuality is capable of expansion to innumerable degrees, in keeping with the degree of infinity which pertains to every soul; it is as foolish to equate it with limitation as to equate man with sin.

REASON AND THERMODYNAMICS

Reason has a necessary role in religion, if only because of the need to live out the consequences of one's beliefs, whatever they may be. The appropriate response must, among other things, always be implicitly the rational one, or else the question as to what was appropriate would become unanswerable. Similarly, each value or principle one adheres to must be given an appropriate application wherever there is any occasion for it. This calls for vigilance combined with the relevant rational judgements.

This dependence on reason has consequences for the form taken by revelation and tradition, since revealed truth must therefore be addressed first of all to the faculty of knowing truth as such, the intelligence. Revelation and its tradition thus cannot conflict with reason and intellect, on pain of ceasing to be what they are. Consequently, to seek tactical advantages by appealing to the irrational can only weaken the tradition as a whole.

Nevertheless, reason is implicitly denied in much modern religion, particularly where it places the emphasis on experiences and relationships rather than on doctrine and moral principles. For the same reason, there is an emphasis on the historical content of revelation, and an avoidance of its moral and doctrinal meaning. The result of this is, as already indicated, that no one can see what, if anything, should result from it in the lives of individuals, apart, of course, from the repetition of the same religious practices. The possibility of increasing spiritual maturity is left to chance, and the overall tendency is toward an effective worship of religion rather than of God. The visible and tangible activities of worship do in fact amount to an acceptable kind of 'God' for increasing numbers of people in today's world, and this includes too many of those who subscribe to orthodox beliefs. The unadmitted substitution of religion for God is also the root cause of all the destructive movements of fanaticism, as well as of many other forms of decadence.

But the role of reason extends beyond matters of analysis, since it concerns the meaning of religious practices as such. The latter are obviously not tied to any directly observable results as a rule, and this can lead to doubts on the grounds that the good achieved by religious practice could result from chance alone. However, the reason for believing that prayer and related practices are always effectual rests on the principle that energy of whatever kind cannot be destroyed, but only transformed and differently directed, as in the laws of thermodynamics. The direction of mental states toward specific purposes in accordance with values is therefore effectual as such, since there is an absolute difference between situations where such acts are made, and those where one remains passive, just as surely as something is more than nothing.

Action of the will is no less action because it is indirect, and it must eventually accumulate to a point at which it becomes the equivalent of direct action. Nothing more is needed to show that the consistent operation of the will from moment to moment makes an irreversible difference to the course of events, and God thereby allows man to share in the dignity of causality as a foretaste of his ultimate participation in the Divine creative power.

All morally-qualified actions involve the direction of volitional energies into realms where they might equally well not have gone. Whatever is once given some degree of being has thence some causal power, and this shows how deeply the creative power is involved in religion. Its beliefs and values are in no way a collection of static objects, as sceptics suppose. There is no hard line between what is, and what is made-to-be.

It is not to the point to object that only God can answer prayer and reward virtue, because the working of a law like the above is nothing if not a manifestation of the Divine will, not in particulars, but in regard to our whole state of being. At the basis of all natural laws is the Uniformity of Nature, the principle that the same kind of effect always follows from the same kind of cause. This is something which no natural forces could ever have brought about or maintain in being for a moment, since their effectiveness depends on it, and not vice-versa. In the light of these reasons, then, religion could be said to be scientific in the best sense of the word, that is, founded on the objective nature of things.

Although it is profoundly rational in itself, therefore, exoteric religion will not identify with a claim to this effect, because in practice it has equally great social and political problems with claims that it is rational and with claims that it is not rational. Hard theoretical alternatives in religion are not the concern of the general public. But for esoteric knowledge, the above ideas are more than enough to reveal a common ground between religion and philosophy, and to show that there is no necessary conflict between them.

THE DIVINE ILLUMINATION OF MIND

What has been said in regard to natural laws applies also to the laws of mind and the ways in which it arrives at knowledge. Just as natural forces cannot create the law that they must invariably act in the same way, so likewise the mind cannot ensure that rational thought must connect with truth by mere effort. Normally, this happens with a tolerable frequency, but this can easily be shown to require something more than the actions of thinking hard and concentrating one's thoughts on a certain result, and that regardless of the extent of one's intelligence.

If, at a given time, I do not know the truth about X, the most I can do is to think about the things which seem to be most relevant to X in the hope that my thought will finally connect with the truth by an association of ideas. It is all too clear, however, that this result cannot be forced, whether it be a minor practical problem, or a problem in a major body of theory. When the mind is applied in a general way to a given object, something else must always happen if this act is to reach a new piece of knowledge; the gap between knowing and not knowing must be closed by something more than the mere will-to-know, and this is in no way under our control.

This is the paradox which Plato solved by means of his analogy with the sun and its light in relation to things visible to our eyes.[1] Eyes and objects together in darkness yield no perception. There has to be light, falling on both the eyes and the objects they see. Similarly, the mind and intelligible realities need the interposition of a third reality, which Plato calls the Good. The Good is the ultimate cause, firstly of the existence of the things known, and secondly of their intelligibility, and thirdly of the mind's reception of them as truths. As light is in a sense a nobler thing than our eyes and their objects, so is the Good a nobler reality than either the intelligence or its intelligibles. This is so because the Good, or God, unlike light, comprises in a higher unity the realities which we find dividedly in our faculties and in the various truths they contain.

What this amounts to is a way of saying that all acts of knowledge are implicitly a conversation with God, an idea which, after Plato's time, became associated with St.Augustine. The necessity of the Divine unifying power means that intellectual work is *per se* God-centered, regardless of its subject and the conscious intentions of those who engage in it. Few things more reveal the blindness of many supposedly intelligent minds than the fact that they cannot realize this and profit spiritually from their own intellectual labours. Their implicit belief that they are the creators of their own knowledge is only a little less absurd than believing that one is one's own creator.

It may be that the relation to God which this involves need not be consciously personal, but conversely, it is a very close one in any case,

1. Plato, *Republic* VI, 508–509.

whether its potential is realized or not. But given the right intention, the pursuit of wisdom can become the basis of a conscious relation to God. Under these conditions, according to Aquinas:

> It is the most sublime (pursuit) because thereby especially does man approach to a likeness to God, Who 'made all things in wisdom,' wherefore since likeness is the cause of love, the pursuit of wisdom especially unites man to God by friendship.[2]

Wisdom is more than knowledge, not least because it is thanks to the disposition of wisdom that ideas are felt as well as known, so that they are able to act directly on one's will, and become normal parts of one's motivation. Given such motivation, the love of wisdom is made real in act. This contrasts with the purely natural condition where the will is moved only by feelings connected with personal desires and aversions. The liberation of the will from sense alone, by effective connection to intellect can result in an intuitive knowledge of 'the one thing needful,' despite its being hard to define. Such knowledge enters into the perfection of the personality.

The perfection proper to mankind is not the same as the perfection proper to God, because it cannot efface the distinction between the created and the Uncreated. Nevertheless, human perfection is in its own way absolute, and means being a co-creator with God, sharing in the universal act by which all things are sustained in being and brought to their fullest fruition.

---

2. Aquinas: *Selected Writings* 6, p53, M.C. D'Arcy, ed.

APPENDIX

ON PROVIDENCE

Since the idea of Providence has been invoked frequently, I will include some sources which serve to define it. In the *Summa*, Aquinas says that Providence is the equivalent in God of the human virtue of prudence and long-term planning:

> This planning or Providence is eternal, though its implementation and management takes place in time. Providence is an act of mind, but one which presupposes the willing of a goal, for no one decides how to achieve a goal unless they want it.... God does not use intermediaries to plan anything, but attends to everything himself in the smallest detail. He implements his plan and manages the world through intermediaries, not because he lacks power in himself, but because in his abundant goodness he wants to share the dignity of cause with creatures. That God has planned everything does not make it happen necessarily. Rather, he plans infallible causes for events that must occur, and fallible causes for events that may or may not. *Must be* and *may not be* are modes of being as such, and thus subject to God's universal providence and plan for the whole of existence, though to no lesser prudence.[1]

According to the same tradition, Providence is:

> God Himself considered in that act by which in His wisdom He so orders all events within the universe that the end for which it was created may be realized. That end is that all creatures should manifest the glory of God, and in particular that man should glorify Him.

---

1. *Summa Theologiae*, chap. 2, 22, 1, Timothy McDermott, ed.

God preserves the universe in being; He acts in and with every creature in each and all of its activities. In spite of sin, which is due to the wilful perversion of human liberty, acting with the concurrence but contrary to the purpose and intention of God, and in spite of evil which is a consequence of sin, He directs all, even evil and sin itself, to the final end for which the universe was created. All these operations on God's part, with the exception of creation, are attributed in Catholic theology to Divine Providence.[2]

Finally, there is Proclus, for whom it rules all things, but in diverse ways, that is, directly over intellectual beings, and indirectly over those subject to the realm of necessity, which is ruled proximately by the mediation of intellect, in a hierarchy of powers in which the higher is the more inclusive:

For the word Providence (*pronoia*) indicates that energy which is prior to that of intellect, and which it is necessary to attribute to *the good* alone; for this alone is more divine than intellect, because much-honoured intellect desires good (i.e., does not have it primally)...while at the same time, he [Plato] exalts intellect, and determines that it rules over necessity. If therefore Providence is above intellect, it is evident that it rules over intellect, and those things which are under this necessity; and that necessity alone rules over those things which are under its dominion.[3]

2. *Catholic Encyclopedia*, 1911 edition, vol. 12.
3. *On Providence and Fate*, [5], [8].

INDEX

Breinigsville, PA USA
08 October 2010
246958BV00001B/77/A